P9-CKS-564

May, 1986

William —
For discussion —
Helen

THE
MILLIONAIRES
OF
GENESIS

Books by CATHERINE PONDER

Healing:
THE DYNAMIC LAWS OF HEALING
THE HEALING SECRET OF THE AGES

Love:
THE PROSPERING POWER OF LOVE

Prayer:
PRAY AND GROW RICH

Prosperity:
THE DYNAMIC LAWS OF PROSPERITY
THE PROSPERITY SECRET OF THE AGES
OPEN YOUR MIND TO PROSPERITY
THE SECRET OF UNLIMITED SUPPLY

The Millionaires of The Bible Series:

THE MILLIONAIRES OF GENESIS . . .
Their Prosperity Secrets For You

THE MILLIONAIRE MOSES . . .
His Prosperity Secrets For You

THE MILLIONAIRE JOSHUA . . .
His Prosperity Secrets For You

THE MILLIONAIRE FROM NAZARETH . . .
His Prosperity Secrets For You

THE MILLIONAIRES OF GENESIS

THEIR PROSPERITY SECRETS FOR YOU!

CATHERINE PONDER

"THE MILLIONAIRES OF THE BIBLE"
Series

Published by
DeVORSS & COMPANY
P.O. Box 550, Marina del Rey, Ca. 90291

Copyright © 1976
by Catherine Ponder

Second Printing, 1979

Library of Congress Catalog Card No. 76-19843

ISBN: 0-87516-215-0

Printed in the United States of America by
Book Graphics, Inc., Marina del Rey, Ca. 90291

CONTENTS

Why Adam is called "the first millionaire." Every man a millionaire! How a sick, penniless man became a millionaire. The prosperity lesson we learn from Adam. How man emerges from a hard-work consciousness. Why call man a millionaire? Are you afraid of the word "millionaire"? The magic word for wealth. How wealth came to her out of the ethers. How to claim your millionaire heritage. Rich ideas, not hard work, bring fortunes. How $20,000 came to her. How a drug addict moved toward healing. From $12,000 to a $25,000 income. How her dental problems were healed. How substance brought $2500, then doubled our income. Prosperity during a recession. How to increase your income with this millionaire meditation.

Abraham's millionaire background. Abraham studied at a prosperity academy. Abraham was an aristocrat. The uplifted state of mind prospers. How to go from competitive to creative prosperity. Schoolteacher went from competitive to creative prosperity. How to get out of stress and strain. How a chiropractor prospered. Vast benefits of the creative level of prosperity. Why you should form a vacuum. How forming a vacuum prospered them. Why some people are never permanently prospered. How forgiveness brought quarter of a million dollars and healing of incurable condition. She became a millionaire through forgiveness. How an artist sold his "$200 dog." When you are ready for this success technique, nothing else will work. How you can manifest supply through pictures. How divorcee and her family prospered through picturing. How picturing prospered an insurance executive. How a realtor raised money for an investment. How to protect your prosperity. How to be lavishly prospered. How he went from $1000 annually to $100,000 annually. The Hebrews' secret name for prosperity. How they went from rags to riches. A millionaire promise to you.

  His Prosperity Secrets For You

How your prosperity can become an automatic process. How to overcome lawsuits, bankruptcy, and other severe financial problems. Meet the mystical millionaire within you. Early psychologists knew about this mystical millionaire. How to activate this mystical millionaire. How they activated great wealth with this method. Why you are master of substance and vast wealth. How the mystical millionaire can prosper you. How to multiply money. A formula that can prosper you mightily. How his second million came more easily. A businessman's million dollar formula. Why her prosperity stopped. How she paid off $9000 indebtedness. How a housewife came into a large inheritance. Where you give is important. How wrong distribution of tithes caused financial problems. The ancient law on where to give. When they held back, it was withheld from them. How tithing brings a job. Why the Hebrew priests were millionaires. Do not apologize when you become a millionaire.

  His Prosperity Secrets For You

The prospering power of joy. The prospering power of peace. The prospering power of beauty. How a Palm Beach apartment came to me. How I moved into the most beautiful office building in town. How Isaac manifested his "wells of abundance." Gerar, a halting place. Isaac's first and second wells of abundance. How these wells of abundance can have an electrifying effect upon your life! How to break the seals on your wells of abundance. How they broke the seals on their wells of abundance. Isaac's third well of abundance. Isaac's fourth well of abundance. The prospering power of agreement. How a businesswoman prospered through agreement. How a businessman prospered through agreement. How the power of agreement worked on a complaining wife. How cruelty in marriage was healed. Agreeing with a former marriage brings a happy new one. How a bereaved woman got a job through the prospering power of agreement. A mental treatment for invoking the prospering power of agreement.

Jacob's problems began because of prosperity. The prospering power of release comes first. How release brought the gift of a grand piano. The prospering power of getting definite. The prospering power of dwelling upon substance. Karmic debts must be paid in order to prosper. How picturing made them rich. How a father made a comeback after his daughter's death. How to claim your freedom from experiences you've outgrown. First comes release, then vast improvement. How inner success must be balanced with outer results. At the height of his wealth, Jacob gave thanks. How a housewife and a man in retirement prospered. Jacob's later years were spent amid vast wealth. The basic success secret you learn from Jacob's life. Why brilliant people may have human relations problems. How to realize your heart's desire.

Jacob's success covenant. Why a success covenant works. How to make a success covenant. How the written word helps a doctor to succeed. Why you should get specific. Why by-passing Part II brings failure. How success covenant works for a musician. Tourist business prospers through success covenant. How a lawyer's success covenant prospered him. You can test a success covenant in small ways first. Other ways of invoking Part II of the covenant. How to assure your prosperity.

Joseph's prosperous background. Specific secrets for gaining
enormous wealth. From $10,000 to $100,000 a year income; how
she maintained it. Why you should keep quiet about what you
picture. How Joseph's prosperity consciousness expanded in Egypt;
how yours can, too. The prosperity lessons Joseph learned from
Potiphar. The prospering power of injustice. The prospering
power of discipline. Two secrets for getting results through picturing. Life as a billionaire. The prospering power of forgiveness.
Lavish abundance during 7 years of plenty. The riches that a
famine brought. The prosperous power of giving, and of giving
thanks. The greatest prosperity secret of all. A billionaire meditation. Instructions for making a prosperity map or wheel of
fortune.

Prosperity begins in Bethlehem. Lack always manifests in the
land of Moab. How a widow happily remarried after leaving
Moab. The prosperity lesson that Naomi learned. How a teacher
demonstrated prosperity for herself and others. Physical form is
the lowest form of energy. How a businessman got out of Moab
and made $15,000. How to pay the bills and taxes, get a home or
job, sell property or get efficient employees. How an army officer
and a businessman prospered. How to develop "a millionaire meditation consciousness." How several thousand dollars came to me.
How a businesswoman became a millionaire. How a housewife
demonstrated financial independence. Prosperous reasons why
Ruth went to Bethlehem. Gathering your good bit by bit leads to
wealth. From one room in Alabama to a famed actor's former
home in California. How Ruth became the first millionairess. The
prospering power of blessing. The prospering power of getting
specific. The prospering power of sorrow. Their happy ending can
be yours too!

Introduction to
THE MILLIONAIRES OF GENESIS

HOW THEY HAVE PROSPERED OTHERS
HOW THEY HAVE PROSPERED THE AUTHOR
HOW THEY CAN PROSPER YOU

How They Have Prospered Others

A salesman went from a $12,000-a-year job to a $25,000-a-year job in just 6 weeks! A formerly unemployed man became a wealthy business executive. A schoolteacher retired early from years of grinding hard work and became financially independent as a writer. A housewife overcame a nervous breakdown and was able to return to her profession, even though she had been told she would never be able to work again.

A lawyer sold 2 pieces of property: One had been for sale for 7 long years. The other piece had not sold for more than 2 years. A businessman was saved from bankruptcy, then prospered in a new career. A man in retirement doubled his income. *All* of these results—and many more—came from learning the prosperity secrets of the millionaires of Genesis, as described in this book.

A number of men and women have reported that they became literal millionaires after learning the prosperity methods of these ancient millionaires.

How They Have Prospered Me

You have probably regarded a millionaire as one who has a million dollars or more, but in its root the word "millionaire" means "abundance *and* happiness." Increased health, wealth, happiness, and spiritual understanding are *all* possible when you begin to use the prosperity secrets of the millionaires of Genesis.

When I began to give my "millionaire seminars," based on the material found in this book, skeptics would ask, "What are your credentials for speaking on this subject? Are *you* a millionaire?"

My reply has always been, "You bet I am!" It might startle my banker to hear me make that claim, so let me explain. I have been studying the millionaires of Genesis and ferreting out their prosperity secrets for many years. Compared to the meager living-in-one-room existence I was experiencing at the time I began my original research for this book, I can assure you that by comparison, then and now, my life has been immeasurably enriched and blessed.

I began to do research on the millionaires of Genesis during the famous recession of 1958, when I was asked to teach a prosperity class to a group of business people in Birmingham, Alabama. That was considered one of the worst economic periods since World War II.

The startling prosperity results obtained by that group of people—right in the midst of unemployment, bread lines, and "hard times" talk—were so impressive that they asked me to begin writing about the power of prosperous thinking. My first book, "The Dynamic Laws of Prosperity,"* was the result. It has gone through many printings and a popular paperback edition continues to reach thousands.

At the time of that 1958 recession, I had been widowed for some time and my young son and I were living in one room. I was overworked and underpaid and we were barely surviving. To all appearances our future looked pretty hopeless.

Yet, as a result of the prosperity secrets I learned from the millionaires of Genesis, I moved from that one-room-existence in Alabama to a greater understanding and a better way of life, first in Texas, and more recently in Southern California. Like Jacob, who became the "persistent millionaire," I had some setbacks along the way (as described in some of my books), but perseverance has brought me through to a victorious way of life.

I am now grateful to be living in the beautiful Palm Desert-Palm Springs area, long called "the playground of the rich." I reside in a celebrity neighborhood where such famous show business personalities as Al Jolson, Gloria Swanson, and Cary Grant have owned homes. My house was reportedly once owned by a popular entertainer who has become a millionaire many times over. I now live and work in an atmosphere of lush tropical beauty. Such surroundings are a vast inspiration to me as I continue to develop and write on the power of prosperous thinking.

The Dynamic Laws of Prosperity by Catherine Ponder was published in 1962 by Prentice-Hall, Inc., Englewood Cliffs, New Jersey.

I hasten to add that there has been no flash flood of supply for me. Only gradually, as I have expanded my thinking and expectations, has my world been enriched. I still arise most mornings before dawn to meditate upon Universal Abundance, and to work at my desk. I continue to travel extensively in order to share with others the results of my continuing research on the fascinating subject of prosperity. Since success is progressive, there is much greater abundance and happiness still to come on all levels of my life as I persist in using the success principles described in this book.

As you learn and apply the prosperity secrets of the millionaires of Genesis, similar blessings and much more can come to you!

How The Millionaires of Genesis Can Prosper You

"I have figured out an easy way to become a millionaire. Please pray with me that one million people will send me one dollar each," someone wrote to me.

People often think as did this person: That wealth can come to them only when other people and conditions respond to them. However, the secret of wealth is that it begins *within* your own thoughts and feelings. Through the deliberate action of your mind, you can develop a millionaire consciousness that will lead you to literal wealth as well as to increased abundance in all phases of your life.

It is appropriate that the millionaires of Genesis show you how this can be done because the word "Genesis" means "to begin," "to initiate action," "to take the first step" or "to get something going."

Abraham, Isaac, Jacob, and Joseph became literal millionaires through deliberate use of the power of prosperous thinking. As they passed on their prosperity secrets to succeeding generations, the Hebrews became one of the wealthiest groups of people the world has ever known.

Their success philosophy was not new. It was known and taught secretly in ancient times. Abraham learned it from the affluent Babylonians, while he lived in the City of Ur. He passed it on to his descendants. Later this success philosophy was reportedly taught for several centuries in the famous School of Philosophy in Alexandria. Well-known psychic Edgar Cayce has spoken of this School in his numerous psychic readings. Bible historians mention it often.

This book points out to you the prosperity secrets which the ancient millionaires used in the secret-success-symbology that cloaked the metaphysical mysticism of the Bible.* In this enlightened Age, the world is again ready to know and use this age-old prosperity teaching so long guarded and offered only to the supposedly "illumined" few.

The millionaire consciousness, developed and enjoyed by the great people of Genesis, is still available to you today!

Why You Should Develop Your Millionaire Consciousness

Why should you develop your millionaire consciousness which includes abundance and happiness? Because the word "desire" in its root means "of the Father." A desire for increased abundance in your life is a normal, God-given desire. It is a universal desire and it should be *expressed con-*

---

*Bible passages quoted herein are from the American Standard Version, and the King James Versions of the Bible.

structively, rather than *su*pressed *de*structively, in order for you to expand your thinking and your world.

An expanded prosperity consciousness is also a necessity in this age of increasing economic demands. Rising prices, "inflationary recessions," and uncertain political and economic world conditions are all indications that we must raise and expand our consciousness to a new level of universal supply. The ancient millionaires in this book show you how to do so.

Prosperous Results May Come To You Within 24 Hours

People who have used the methods described in this book have often gotten prosperous results within 24 hours! The same thing may happen to you as you get busy using the techniques offered you by the millionaires of Genesis. Even if results take longer, you will find it a satisfying experience to begin applying their success techniques in your own life.

As stated earlier, the word "millionaire" means not only "a million or more" but also "abundance and happiness." As you invoke the prosperity laws used by the ancient millionaires, you will begin to develop your millionaire consciousness in an over-all way. Such a practice assures you of increased abundance *and* happiness.

My Millionaire Invitation To You

Yes, the millionaires of Genesis have been good friends of mine because they helped me break out of a hard shell of life-long poverty, and gradually grow into a happy, fulfilling way of life. And they have done the same for many others.

As you join me in getting mentally acquainted with them,

I trust that these ancient millionaires may become some of the best friends you have ever known too! I invite you to write me of your experiences in increased health, wealth, and happiness as you use their age-old methods. It is a rewarding lifetime process. Be assured that I will be using their prosperity secrets right along with you.

CATHERINE PONDER

P.O. Drawer 1278
Palm Desert, Ca., 92260
U.S.A.

THE FIRST MILLIONAIRE--
ADAM

HIS PROSPERITY SECRETS FOR YOU

— Chapter 1 —

A minister once visited a lady who had studied the power of thought for more than 50 years. Yet he found her in a very sad condition.

She said to him, "Young man, do not make the mistake I made, and do not let others make this mistake. When I began studying the power of thought, I felt I was 'too spiritual' to include a study of the principles of prosperity, so I ignored that subject. I studied the power that thought has in relation to prayer, healing, and other facets of life; and I was helped tremendously through my study. But you see my condition today. Here I am—a student of mind power of 50 years' standing. Yet I am living in one room on a bare existence level. I now realize my mistake in not studying and practicing the laws of prosperity. How I have cheated myself."

Like everything else, the subject of prosperity unfolds to those who study its laws and persist in practicing them, both inwardly and outwardly. The millionaires of Genesis show you how, beginning with Adam.

Why Adam Is Called "The First Millionaire"

Adam is described as "the first millionaire" because his prosperity story is found in the early chapters of Genesis. He might also be considered "the allegorical millionaire." The first 11 chapters of Genesis are considered symbolic allegories or legends which were universally known to the ancient people long before the time of the Hebrews.

These ancient allegories contained some of the greatest success symbology known to man. That is doubtless why the prosperous-minded Moses included them in the Book of Genesis, even though these same legends are also found in the sacred writings of Egypt, Chaldea, and other nations which flourished thousands of years before the time of the Hebrews. Not until the 12th chapter of Genesis, beginning with the story of Abraham, does the literal history of the Bible begin.

Every Man A Millionaire!

In literal terms, a "millionaire" is considered a very wealthy person—one worth at least one thousand thousand dollars. Economists explain that there are "rich millionaires" and "poor millionaires." A "poor millionaire" is a person who has *only* a million dollars or more. A "rich millionaire" is one with *at least* a hundred million or more.

Since Adam of the Creation Story symbolizes Every Man,

then every person has that same millionaire heritage which God bestowed upon Adam.

You will find the formula for becoming a millionaire in the early chapters of Genesis. When you read it carefully, you will discover that the Creation Story is a prosperity story. It is a description of lavish abundance.

But it goes further. After the world was grandly created, containing lavish abundance, then Jehovah created man in His own image as a spiritual being. Man was given dominion over this world of abundance. (Genesis 1:26-28) At this point he would doubtless have been considered a "rich millionaire."

For centuries there have been those who have said that Adam was a "miserable sinner" because he was formed from "the dust of the earth" according to a later accounting. (Genesis 2:7) But don't you believe it!

The "dust of the earth" from which Adam was formed symbolizes the rich, radiant, unlimited substance out of which the whole universe was formed. Adam, symbolizing every person, formed from "the dust of the earth" means that you are radiant substance and so am I! We have a millionaire-heritage as did Adam—even that of becoming "rich millionaires!"

How A Sick, Penniless Man Became A Millionaire

In the 1920's a sick, penniless man learned this ancient secret that had been bestowed upon Adam. He began to declare to himself every day, "I AM THE RICH, RADIANT SUBSTANCE OF THE UNIVERSE. I AM. I AM. I AM. MY MIND, BODY, AND FINANCIAL AFFAIRS ARE NOW FILLED WITH THIS RICH UNIVERSAL SUBSTANCE. EVERY PHASE OF MY LIFE IS NOW

BLESSED WITH THIS RADIANT SUBSTANCE." The results?

First, this man was healed physically. Then he got a job. As he continued privately to call on the unlimited substance of the universe to bless his world, he was given a sum of money by a friend, who suggested he invest it. He did, and his investment grew. Just prior to the great Depression, his friend suggested he reinvest what he had accumulated in certain stocks that were considered secure even by the super-rich Rockefellers, Fords, and DuPonts. He did so, and prospered right through the Depression. Soon he was almost as "rich as Rockefeller." He has continued to enjoy his wealth until this day. It all began the day he started to call on universal substance to prosper and to heal him.

The Prosperity Lesson We Learn From Adam

The prosperity lesson we quickly learn from that first millionaire, the allegorical Adam, is that he misused his mind powers and fell from his heritage of vast abundance. When he dwelled upon a belief in evil—lack and limitation—even though he was surrounded by lavish abundance, "Jehovah sent him forth from the Garden of Eden to till the ground from whence he was taken." (Genesis 3:22, 23)

Most of us can identify with Adam. Perhaps you have goofed in the same way he did. You may have been tempted to dwell upon a belief in lack and limitation, even though you obviously live in a world of vast abundance. If so, you may have found yourself tilling the ground from whence you came.

However, it's not as bad as it sounds. That "ground" from which Adam was taken symbolizes the substance of the universe. To "till it" means to begin using the inner laws of prosperity—as described in this book—to bring abundant supply into your life again.

The good news is that you do not have to remain in the "hard work consciousness" into which Adam fell.

How Man Emerges From A Hard-Work Consciousness

How does man's body and world emerge as radiant substance? How does he get out of a hard-work consciousness?

When you begin to use your mind to think and act prosperously again, you evolve out of a hard work consciousness into a world of increasing abundance. In its oldest form the word "man" means "mind." Man *is* mind. Man is mind power.

It is through your mind power that you can generate the radiant, luminous substance which is the basis of your world. *It is through the mind that you can claim your millionaire heritage of lavish abundance.*

All great philosophers and metaphysicians have known this. In ancient legends, Adam was described as a "luminous being," his body composed of a "kind of radiance." Plato talked about man being "luminous substance."

As pointed out previously, the description of man's creation is found in the Book of Genesis, and the word "Genesis" means "becoming or emerging." This means that you and I are in a constant process of becoming or emerging as radiant substance when we recognize it with our minds.

Why Call Man A Millionaire?

You may be thinking, "Why do you call man a millionaire? Why can't you be satisfied with calling him a potentially prosperous being?"

Let us face the truth honestly: Man seeks unlimited bounty! It is an innate desire in every normal person. Nothing can possibly satisfy anybody short of unlimited supply. Why should it, once you learn that there is no limit to the bounty of substance and that, through the action of your mind, you can form it in unlimited amounts out of the ethers of this rich universe?

In my own growth out of poverty into a gradually increasing affluence, I have found that the more I employed the inner laws of prosperity and unfolded their abundance, the more I desired even greater prosperity and the beauty and freedom that are a part of it. My experience appears to be a universal one among those who are also on the path of prosperous thinking.

So be honest and admit that you seek unlimited bounty; that nothing short of unlimited supply can possibly satisfy you. Admit that this is mentally and emotionally healthy— that it is normal and right for you!

A loving Father thought of it first and provided a lavish universe of unlimited substance. He then gave you a mind with which to claim it. God is just as much the Provider for His children as He is the Healer. That the Lord can provide for you is just as much a Bible promise as that the Lord can heal you. You should not get mixed up with the idea of lack any more that you should get mixed up with the thought of sickness. Substance owns all things.

Are You Afraid Of The Word "Millionaire"?

Knowing this, you can stop apologizing for the use of the word "millionaire" in this book. You can even stop trying to tone down that word, if you want to unleash in your own life the abundance that is yours by divine right.

I once gave one of my "millionaire seminars" to a group of business and professional people in a church. They talked about becoming "spiritual millionaires" as though there was something wrong with becoming financial millionaires. I am not sure the people in that church will ever become millionaries of *any* description. They were much too afraid of the word!

Later I gave that same "millionaire seminar" in another church to a similar group. The people in that class did not flinch when I talked about the millionaires of the Bible, and how we are all potential millionaires.

One reason the word "millionaire" did not bother them may have been because there were at least 30 millionaires attending that seminar! Of course, they may have been "poor millionaires" with *only* a million or so, trying to become "rich millionaires." In any event, they had no psychological blocks against the word.

The Magic Word For Wealth

Here is one of the first prosperity secrets we learn from the early millionaires: The Bible describes man's wealth often in terms of "substance." The word "substance" was a magic word for wealth in Bible times.

The wealth of Abraham and Lot was described: "Their substance was great." (Genesis 13:6) Joseph's wealth was described: "He (King Pharaoh) made him (Joseph) lord of his house, And ruler of all his substance." (Psalms 105: 21) Job's vast wealth was described in terms of substance. (Job 1) King David appointed stewards to take care of "all substance." (I Chronicles 28:1) Solomon advised his followers in the Proverbs: "Honor Jehovah with thy substance, and with the first fruits of all thine increase. So shall thy barns be filled with plenty and thy vats shall overflow with new wine." (Proverbs 3:9, 10) The Bible speaks of God giving King Hezekiah "very much substance." (II Chronicles 32:29) And the prophet made a great prosperity statement when he said even in jest, "I am become rich, I have found me out substance." (Hosea 12:8) Jesus described the poverty that came upon the Prodigal Son when he wasted his "substance" in riotous living. (Luke 15:13)

However, the prospering power of the word "substance" dates back much earlier than Bible times. The cultured classes among the ancient Egyptians knew that there was only one substance underlying everything, but the Egyptians carefully guarded this secret. They felt it would be unwise for the common laborers to learn that the substance which was used to build the fabled Pyramids was the same substance which the priests used to perform their feats of magic.

In studying the prosperity symbology of the Bible, you quickly discover that *the Bible is a study in substance and how to mold it into tangible abundance.* The millionaires of Bible times knew that substance was the basis of all wealth. They knew how to mold it into prosperous results through their thoughts, words, and actions.

For instance, the Hebrews worked long and hard to get into the Promised Land of Canaan. Metaphysically the word "Canaan" means "realm of substance." They were trying to get into their Promised Land of substance. They were trying to gain an understanding of substance and how to manifest it as visible results. That they did learn this age-old secret is evidenced by the fact that they became one of the wealthiest groups of people the world has ever known. As you use their success secrets, which are both literal and symbolic, you can move forward toward your Promised Land of rich, unlimited substance, too!

How Wealth Came To Her Out Of The Ethers

Some of the ancient people gained such an understanding of substance that they could produce whatever they wanted right out of the ethers. Jesus did so on a number of occasions as He manifested "instant loaves and fishes," "instant wine," and "instant tax money."

A select few down through the ages have been able to do this. During the 16th, 17th, and 18th centuries in Europe and Asia, there were sages and adepts who could manifest money instantly. In the Far East the Holy Men have been doing this for centuries.

A friend once related that she had studied the subject of substance over a period of time until she was finally able to cause a gold piece to appear right out of the ethers. It became visible on the floor by the chair where she often sat and meditated. She kept this lovely gold piece in her home for some time. Finally it faded away again. But that was not the end of her story.

As she continued declaring that substance was the basis of all her supply, she became a very wealthy woman with property, investments, and money in a number of banks. These assets did not fade away. She enjoyed them for the rest of her life.

How To Claim Your Millionaire Heritage

Perhaps you are thinking, "But what does this subject of 'substance' have to do with my millionaire heritage?"

The better you undersand the nature of substance out of

*which all wealth comes, the better you will be able to bring
forth whatever you desire, and the better every phase of your
life will be!* All of the substance out of which your home,
friends, health, and wealth are made is within you and all
around you. It begins to manifest for you when you recognize it and call upon it for help.

The word "substance" means "that which stands under"
all visible forms of life. Metaphysicians have described it
as "the body of God" out of which all things are formed
through the action of the mind.

Why haven't more people become wealthy if they are
surrounded, even filled, with this rich substance of the universe?

Because substance is passive. It waits for you to deliberately mold it and shape it through your prosperous thoughts,
words, acts. In the very beginning man was given dominion over this visible world of lavish abundance, as well as
over the invisible world of unlimited substance. It is up to
you to definitely claim it.

"In simple terms, how do I deliberately contact this universal substance and make it mine as increased wealth?"
you may be asking.

Through your words! You can begin to claim your mil-
lionaire heritage by declaring that you are substance, that
the universe is substance, that by your spoken words you
are forming that substance into tangible results. You can
begin now by declaring daily: "DIVINE SUBSTANCE
IS THE ONE AND ONLY REALITY IN MY FINAN-
CIAL AFFAIRS NOW. DIVINE SUBSTANCE HEALS
ME. DIVINE SUBSTANCE PROSPERS ME. DIVINE
SUBSTANCE ESTABLISHES ORDER IN MY LIFE
AND FINANCIAL AFFAIRS NOW."

Rich Ideas, Not Hard Work, Bring Fortunes

If you have been one of those well-meaning people who has gotten into the Adam consciousness of hard work, thinking that to be your salvation from lack—or if you have erroneously believed that hard work alone would bring you riches—you are in for a pleasant surprise! Wealth—especially vast wealth—rarely comes as a result of back-breaking work. Fortunes are the result of rich ideas. The idea that can help you experience increased wealth is the idea of "substance."

How $20,000 Came To Her

There once was a lady who needed $20,000. She began to declare every day, "I AM ALL THE SUBSTANCE THERE IS. I AM DIVINE SUBSTANCE." Within a few weeks the money came through an investment that paid off unexpectedly.

How A Drug Addict Moved Toward Healing

The thought of "divine substance" brings increased good in all phases of life. A drug addict attended a prosperity lecture in which the speaker declared that man is radiant substance, and that man should daily claim his heritage of radiant substance. At the close of the lecture everyone attending affirmed together that they were radiant substance, and that the rich substance of the universe was the one and only reality in their lives and affairs.

Later an usher found a large vial of drugs sitting on top of one of the seats. It was too large to have fallen accidentally out of a coat pocket. Obviously it had been left on the seat deliberately. Some person attending that lecture had decided to claim his heritage and prove that he was master of substance, thereby claiming his healing from drug addiction.

The substance idea can help you claim your freedom from unwanted conditions of mind, body, affairs, or relationships. Divine substance has a universal power and a universal appeal for good in your life when you recognize it and call on it for help. The ancient people knew the power of thinking about substance and affirming it, thereby manifesting health, wealth, and happiness. You can too!

From A $12,000 to A $25,000 Income

A businessman, who was dissatisfied with his $12,000 a year income, began to declare daily, "I AM SURROUNDED BY DIVINE SUBSTANCE, AND THIS DIVINE SUBSTANCE MANIFESTS A LARGE FINANCIAL INCOME FOR ME NOW." Within 6 weeks he was offered a $25,000 a year job!

He had not even gone out looking for this job. It was offered him through a long-distance telephone call from the Board Chairman of a large corporation. He accepted it gladly.

How Her Dental Problems Were Healed

A schoolteacher in England learned that she was master of substance. She began to declare daily, "I AM MASTER OF SUBSTANCE. THEREFORE I HAVE GOOD TEETH BECAUSE THEY ARE RADIANT SUBSTANCE." Dental problems of long standing began to clear up.

How Substance Brought $2500, Then Doubled
Our Income

Once on a cold day when the financial income of my church had been low, I spent some time declaring, "I INVITE THE POWERFUL, LOVING SUBSTANCE OF THE UNIVERSE TO PRODUCE ABUNDANT SUPPLY HERE AND NOW." The next day a check for $2500 was given to the church. It seemed like a fortune!

On another occasion when the church's financial income had been low, I asked members of my prayer group to meet with me regularly to call on substance to meet our needs. We began to declare at our weekly meetings, "THIS MINISTRY IS SURROUNDED BY DIVINE SUBSTANCE, AND THIS DIVINE SUBSTANCE MANIFESTS ABUNDANT SUPPLY FOR THIS CHURCH HERE AND NOW."

Things began to improve. Later the accountant informed the church trustees that the income had doubled that year, even though our financial needs had been kept secret. There had been no fund-raising drives, no legacies, no other financial windfalls.

Prosperity During A Recession

A group of business people once decided to test the prospering power of substance during a recession. They agreed privately to declare each day: "DIVINE SUBSTANCE IS THE ONE AND ONLY REALITY IN MY FINANCIAL AFFAIRS. I PRAISE MY WORLD AS THE PERFECT CREATION OF DIVINE SUBSTANCE, AND I

NOW SEE MORE FINANCIAL INCOME FOR MY-
SELF THAN I HAVE EVER SEEN BEFORE."

The results?

One man's investments on the stock market shot up. He
sold them at a tremendous profit. The owner of a cleaning
plant was able to stay in business and prosper when several
other cleaners nearby went out of business. A doctor, an
engineer, a housewife all had financial demonstrations in
the face of previous financial challenges. An insurance executive, a salesman, a merchant all had new channels of
income open to them.

*How To Increase Your Income With This Millionaire
Meditation*

You can increase your financial income in unlimited ways
as you begin daily to call on the lavish substance of the universe to provide for you. As you praise Divine Substance,
it will respond with increased abundance.

Like Isaac, one of the millionaires of Genesis, you may
even increase your income a hundredfold! (See Chapter 4.)
*That everything has its root in divine substance has been
the millionaire secret of the ages!*

You can begin now to develop your millionaire consciousness by declaring aloud at least 5 minutes a day these statements:

"DIVINE SUBSTANCE CANNOT BE TAKEN FROM
ME NOW. I AM THE RICH, RADIANT SUBSTANCE
OF THE UNIVERSE. I AM MASTER OF SUB-
STANCE, AND I TAKE CONTROL OF SUBSTANCE
IN MY THOUGHTS, WORDS, AND ACTIONS NOW.

DIVINE SUBSTANCE IS THE ONE AND ONLY RE-
ALITY IN MY FINANCIAL AFFAIRS NOW. I PRAISE
MY WORLD AS THE PERFECT CREATION OF DI-
VINE SUBSTANCE, AND I NOW SEE MORE FI-
NANCIAL INCOME FOR MYSELF THAN I HAVE
EVER SEEN BEFORE! I INVITE THE POWERFUL,
LOVING SUBSTANCE OF THE UNIVERSE TO
POUR OUT UNLIMITED WEALTH UPON ME. I
CLAIM MY MILLIONAIRE HERITAGE OF IN-
CREASED HEALTH, WEALTH, AND HAPPINESS
NOW."

SUMMARY

1. God is just as much the Provider for His children as He is their Healer. God is unlimited supply. Spirit owns all things.

2. The Creation Story is a prosperity story. It is a description of lavish abundance.

3. After the world was created in grand style, containing lavish abundance, then man was formed from the "dust of the earth" which was radiant substance. Man as luminous substance was given dominion over the universe through the action of his mind.

4. Adam, symbolizing Every Man, fell from this millionaire consciousness into the hard-work consciousness when he dwelled upon the belief in evil, lack and limitation, even though he was living amid lavish abundance.

5. Man can regain his millionaire heritage by recognizing Divine Substance as the one and only reality and by affirming Divine Substance as the Source of his wealth. The Bible often described man's wealth in terms of "substance."

6. By affirming substance, we release it to work for us. By affirming substance, we regain our millionaire heritage.

7. Substance loves to be recognized. Substance loves to work for us.

8. That everything has its root in divine substance was an ancient teaching. This has been a secret fit for millionaires down through the ages.

9. You can increase your income in unlimited amounts as you begin daily to declare that Divine Substance is the one and only reality in your financial affairs now. Persist in recognizing Divine Substance as the foundation of your wealth.

THE PIONEERING MILLIONAIRE--
ABRAHAM

HIS PROSPERITY SECRETS FOR YOU

— Chapter 2 —

When I first mentioned in a lecture that Abraham was a millionaire, a startled Texan asked, "*If* Abraham was a millionaire, how many oil wells did he have?"

"I don't know, but I will find out," was my reply. When I checked the description of Abraham's wealth in the Book of Genesis, I could not locate a single oil well for him. But as I studied carefully the passages describing his wealth, one verse stood out: "Abraham was very rich in *cattle,* in silver, and in gold." (Genesis 13:2)

When I happily reported to that skeptical Texan that Abraham had been a rich cattleman, he was so impressed that he decided Abraham was not only a millionaire but a "Texas millionaire" and that Abraham's cattle had probably been "Longhorn steers"—as found in the Lone Star State!

Abraham's Millionaire Background

The history of the Bible, in the 12th chapter of the Book of Genesis, begins by describing the life of Abraham (first called Abram) and his tremendous wealth. We have often thought of Abraham as the Father of the Hebrew people— as a great spiritual leader—which he was. But Abraham also became a man of vast wealth, which the Bible boldly describes.

His background was fabulous. It gave him both a material understanding and a spiritual understanding of prosperity—and how to manifest it in his world.

His life began in the Babylonian City of Ur. The Babylonians were an advanced and prosperous people. By their ingenious techniques in agriculture, commerce, and finance, Babylon's citizens became the richest of their era. It was the wise Babylonians who first developed and practiced the sound financial principles we regard so highly today: Those of insurance, savings, home ownership, investments, and systematic tithing.

It was into this prosperous, advanced civilization that Abraham was born and spent the first 75 years of his life. During this period, he observed those wise business practices of the Babylonians that had led them to vast wealth. As he absorbed the millionaire consciousness of the Babylonians, it gave him a material understanding of wealth and all that it could do to ease life's burdens.

Abraham Studied At A Prosperity Academy

According to ancient lore, during this first period of his life, Abraham also studied in the Academy of Melchizedek. Legend states that Melchizedek was a mystical millionaire, who taught the mental and spiritual laws of prosperity in his Academy. Abraham learned this prosperity teaching and used it throughout his life. This secret instruction gave him a mental and spiritual understanding of prosperity and how to manifest it lavishly.

Abraham Was An Aristocrat

In the past, you may have regarded some of the people of Genesis as native tribesmen, wandering about in the dusty desert. But historians have described Abraham as a learned man and prophet of God, who belonged to a wealthy Babylonian family. They describe him as having a "princely nature," as being a true gentleman of "pioneer aristocracy."

A "pioneer" is one who goes before, preparing the way for others to follow. That's what Abraham did.

During that first period of his life spent in Babylon, Abraham had gained an understanding of the nature of substance and how to manifest it as vast wealth through his thoughts, words, and acts. He had learned that everything has its root in substance—that substance is the basis of all wealth.

The Uplifted State of Mind Prospers

The word "Abraham" in Hebrew means "Father of Height" or "Father of Exaltation." It is the heightened, uplifted, exalted state of mind that is the prospering state of mind. There is absolutely no prospering power, healing power, peace or harmony in a depressed state of mind. Negative, depressed thinking scares the wealth of the universe away from you rather than attracting it to you.

Through the actions of his life, Abraham reveals the secret for developing an uplifted state of mind in which you are able to manifest abundance.

Abraham has been described as "the man of faith." Here is his first prosperity secret: The ancient people knew that *faith moves on substance*. The events of Abraham's life show you how your simple acts of faith can move on the lavish substance of the universe, and manifest it as increased abundance in your world.

How To Go From Competitive To Creative Prosperity

Abraham's first act of faith was to follow the Lord's command to get out of the country he had occupied for 75 years, and to go into a new land in which the Lord promised to bless him, and to make him great. (Genesis 12:1, 2)

His departure from Babylon symbolizes your departure from a material and competitive consciousness of prosperity, and your growth into a creative level of supply through the use of your mind. Many people who are striving to be successful are still in a physical, sweat-of-the-brow, hard-work consciousness. They erroneously believe they must compete for the wealth that is already visible in the world about them—wealth that belongs to someone else.

Abraham's journey into the Land of Canaan symbolizes the development of a creative consciousness of prosperity that does just the opposite; it does not compete for wealth already visible. It dares to create its own new wealth from the invisible substance of the universe through prosperous thoughts, words, and actions. The Land of Canaan symbolizes that rich realm of substance.

Most of us are in the process of growing out of a competitive, hard-work consciousness of prosperity into the creative level of prosperity where we create our prosperity mentally first. In this process, we grow into an understanding of the "realm of substance" in order to get into the Land of Canaan. We learn to mold that rich realm of substance with our prosperous thoughts, words, and acts.

This Land of Canaan that was given to Abraham's heirs by Jehovah for "'an everlasting possession" is a gift to every one of us! (Genesis 17:8) This realm of substance is also your "everlasting possession" which you can claim as you deliberately employ prosperous thoughts, words, and actions!

Schoolteacher Went From Competitive to Creative Prosperity

A schoolteacher learned that she could go from a competitive, hard-work level of prosperity to a creative level. She learned from Abraham that her acts of faith would move on substance and draw far greater prosperity to her than ever before. To help her faith move on substance she began to declare, "I AM NOW SHOWN NEW WAYS OF LIVING AND NEW METHODS OF WORK. I AM NOT CONFINED TO THE WAYS AND METHODS OF THE PAST."

At first nothing happened. As she persisted in declaring these words every day, her work load became lighter, and her working conditions more pleasant. When she continued reminding herself that she did not have to compete for her prosperity, ideas began to come to her and she set them down in articles, which she sold.

This encouraged her to begin setting down more of her ideas in books. Within 2 years, she had prospered to the extent that she was able to retire early from her teaching job. Her statement worked! She *was* shown new ways of living and new methods of work. She is no longer confined to the competitive ways and hard-work methods of the past —and she is far more prosperous.

How To Get Out Of Stress And Strain

The person in a material and competitive consciousness of prosperity would not have dared to do what Abraham did—leave the old country, especially such an affluent one. The person who is in a competitive state of mind depends upon people and conditions for his prosperity. He panics if the people and conditions connected with his prosperity fade out or change. He may try to hang on to them or he may try to force his good in other ways.

Such a person is in a constant uproar over world conditions and economic trends because he feels they control his destiny and that he is subject to them. He feels he is their hopeless, helpless victim. He blames forces outside himself— people and conditions—for all his financial problems of the past or present. His life is a vicious circle of financial uncertainty and strain.

In getting out of the old country, Abraham was trying to show us that we must let go such limited ideas about the Source of our supply. We must recognize that God—not man—is the true Source of all our good.

How A Chiropractor Prospered

A doctor of chiropractic said, "Learning that God is the Source of my supply was the turning point in my life from failure to success. This freed me from depending upon my patients, or from blaming economic conditions when things did not go right."

After he realized the True Source of his wealth, he was able to build a new $100,000 clinic within 8 months. His daily prosperity statement had been, "I DO NOT DEPEND UPON PERSONS OR CONDITIONS FOR MY PROSPERITY. GOD IS THE SOURCE OF MY SUPPLY, AND GOD PROVIDES HIS OWN AMAZING CHANNELS OF PROSPERITY FOR ME NOW." As he continued to affirm God as the Source of his prosperity, people and conditions adjusted to his prosperity consciousness.

Vast Benefits of the Creative Level of Prosperity

On the creative level of prosperity, you work for the joy of it and prosperity flows to you and through you in streams of plenty. Instead of working to make a living, you are busy making a life—which includes so much more.

Going from the competitive to the creative level of prosperity does not mean that you talk down the money idea. Instead you would agree with a friend of mine who says, "Money is Divine Substance dressed up in green pants."

On the creative level of supply, it has been established that prosperity may be the result of 98% mental preparation, and 2% outer action. On the competitive, hard-work level, it is reversed. Man often spins his wheels with too little mental preparation and too much outward action.

Why You Should Form A Vacuum

Like the pioneering millionaire, Abraham, you can get out of the old country by forming a vacuum. You must learn to let go, give up, make room for the things you want and desire. You should always want something better than you now have. That is the urge of progress. It shows development and growth.

Just as children outgrow their clothes, you outgrow your previous ideals and ambitions. You broaden your horizons of life as you expand inwardly and advance outwardly. *There must be a constant elimination of the old to keep pace with your new growth.* If you cling to the old, you hinder your advance, or stop it altogether. This applies to your tangible possessions as well as to your intangible ideals.

You can unblock and undam your good by forming a vacuum. Countless people have done so with amazing results. It is a delightful act of faith that inevitably brings results.

How Forming A Vacuum Prospered Them

A young couple heard about the prospering power of forming a vacuum at an Iowa prosperity seminar I conducted. The wife had always been a "pack rat" and had kept their home filled with many items they no longer used. She decided to form a vacuum by having a "garage sale" at which she sold hundreds of dollars' worth of unused items. This was their first prosperity demonstration.

As they continued to clean up and clean out, the husband was offered the finest job of his life in Denver. A few months later, he and his wife attended my Denver seminar and gave a "prosperity testimonial" explaining how the vacuum law of prosperity had quickly worked for them!

Why Some People Are Never Permanently Prospered

You can also get out of old states of mind and circumstances (symbolized by the old country that Abraham left) by forming a vacuum in an *inner* way, through the practice of forgiveness.

Many people are never permanently prospered, no matter what else they do, because they are holding grudges and negative feelings toward other people. Until they get down to business and forgive, their prosperity does not come because they have not made room for it, mentally or emotionally.

The word "forgive" means "to give up." Forgiveness is not an unpleasant, dramatic, outer act in which you say, "I am sorry," when you are not. Instead, forgiveness is a pleasant inner act which leaves you at peace with yourself and others.

It is wise to give yourself a universal forgiveness treatment every day. This keeps your mind and emotions cleared of negative feelings that can block your good. You might declare daily: "ALL THAT HAS OFFENDED ME, I FORGIVE. WITHIN AND WITHOUT, I FORGIVE. THINGS PAST, THINGS PRESENT, THINGS FUTURE I FORGIVE. I FORGIVE EVERYTHING AND EVERYBODY WHO CAN POSSIBLY NEED FORGIVENESS OF THE PAST OR PRESENT. I FORGIVE POSITIVELY EVERYONE. THEY ARE FREE NOW, AND I AM FREE TOO. ALL THINGS ARE CLEARED UP BETWEEN US NOW AND FOREVER."

How Forgiveness Brought Quarter of A Million Dollars and Healing of Incurable Condition

When you hold resentment toward someone or some condition of the past or present, you are bound to that person or condition by an emotional link that is stronger than steel. This blocks your prosperity, and keeps you tied to the very person or condition you are trying to get free of. The practice of forgiveness is the only way to dissolve that unhappy link and go free to a better life.

A friend in New York began to practice forgiveness daily. So many names and situations of the past and present began to float up in her memory that she made a "forgiveness list" placing each name and situation remembered on it. Daily she spoke words of forgiveness for all the people and situations on her list: "I FULLY AND FREELY FORGIVE YOU. I LOOSE YOU AND LET YOU GO. YOU FULLY AND FREELY FORGIVE ME. YOU LOOSE ME AND LET ME GO. ALL THINGS ARE CLEARED UP BETWEEN US NOW AND FOREVER."

She was very honest. She said it took her a year to forgive some of the names and situations appearing on her list. But it proved to be the most fabulous year of her life! First, a great sense of peace enveloped her and released her from past unhappiness and judgments. Second, she was healed of a supposedly "incurable" health condition. Finally, one of the people she had just spent a year forgiving made her a gift of a quarter of a million dollars!

You can make a "forgiveness list" and begin to practice forgiveness daily in the full assurance that FORGIVENESS HEALS. FORGIVENESS PROSPERS.

She Became A Millionaire Through Forgiveness

A friend in Florida once said, "I know that forgiveness prospers. We have had many hurts in our family, but my sister has refused to accept any of those hurts, or to dwell upon them. The more she has practiced forgiveness, the more wealth has been poured out upon her. My sister is a millionaire today because of forgiveness!"

How Artist Sold His "$200 Dog"

Another way you can get out of old states of mind and circumstances is by writing out what you want eliminated from your life.

An artist had sold one of his paintings to a client who paid him off with a "two hundred dollar dog." The artist was delighted until he realized how much the dog was costing him in time and care: He had to feed him, walk him, entertain him, and take him to the vet for shots. When he decided to sell this pet, he quickly discovered that no one seemed interested in owning such a "high class dog."

Finally he remembered about the power of elimination lists, and wrote down on his list the desire to sell the dog for $200 to someone who would love and appreciate such a fine pet. When he ran an ad (again) in the paper, he got an immediate response. That "two hundred dollar dog" was quickly sold and well placed for exactly that amount.

You do not have to be afraid of the word "eliminate." The function of that word "elimination" is two-fold: Its purpose is *first,* to eliminate error from your life, and *second,* to expand your good. *Elimination of something from your life is always an indication that something better is on the way!* After writing out what you want eliminated from your life, declare daily: "I LET GO AND TRUST." The results can astound you.

When You are Ready For This Success Technique— Nothing Else Will Work

This is what Abraham did when he left posh, elegant Babylon with all of its obvious wealth, and boldly went off to that barren land of Canaan. Abraham intuitively knew that all of your loosing is not simply the loosing of so-called evil.

You must loose forms of good as well when your progress or that of others demands it. Your good is seldom static. It is progressive. It changes and evolves. You must change and evolve with it. In the Land of Canaan Abraham became rich.

But he had something to learn first: Upon arriving in the Land of Canaan, it looked so barren that he left it and decided to try his luck in fertile, prosperous Egypt. Judging from appearances, Abraham had made a wise decision. But he got into trouble in Egypt, and was soon forced to leave and return to the Land of Canaan.

This may happen to you, too, as you begin to develop your millionaire consciousness. Why? Egypt appeared to be a rich land of opportunity, but it symbolizes a material consciousness of prosperity. Abraham only got into trouble in Egypt because he was ready for something more than mere rich appearances of wealth. He was ready to develop an inner understanding of supply—a mental and spiritual one.

Abraham was forced to return to the Land of Canaan— which means "realm of substance—and in that apparently barren place to gain an understanding of divine substance, and how to manifest it through the action of the mind. As he practiced this prosperity method, he gained vast wealth.

Like Abraham, even after you have learned the deeper mental and spiritual laws of prosperity (such as he had allegedly learned at the Academy of Melchizedek in Babylon), you may first attempt to return to old methods of demonstrating prosperity. If so, like Abraham in Egypt, you will quickly discover that they no longer work for you because you are ready to learn how to take hold of invisible substance, even though it looks barren and inadequate to you. You are ready to begin the practice of manifesting that invisible substance as visible results in your life.

Once you learn this inner method, you will never again depend upon the outer competitive methods of supply! Gaining an inner hold on substance and learning how to manifest it as visible supply are fascinating, soul satisfying processes which give you "cosmic security." You will never fear lack again! Abraham proved this when he returned to the Land of Canaan and settled down there. So can you, as you use his methods.

How You Can Manifest Supply Through Pictures

One of the ways that Abraham took hold of invisible substance and manifested it as visible wealth in his life was through the picturing power of the mind. This is an ancient method for demonstrating prosperity.

In the Land of Canaan, he and his nephew increased their wealth rapidly. Finally the land was not able to bear them because their substance was so great. (Genesis 13:6)

Because of strife that arose among their herdsmen, they decided to separate.

Since Abraham was a true gentleman of pioneer aristocracy, he generously offered Lot whatever land he chose. Lot judged according to appearances and took the green, prosperous Plain of Jordan. It was well watered and considered the Garden of the Lord. What Lot did not know was that this Plain of Jordan was filled with warlike tribes. Later, when he got into battle with them, Abraham graciously rescued him.

When Lot had taken what he considered to be the best land, Abraham was left to live in the barren Land of Canaan. Instead of fretting about the apparent wealth that had been taken from him by his ambitious nephew, Abraham graciously released it, and followed the advice of Jehovah: "Lift up now thine eyes, and look from the place where thou art, northward and southward, eastward and westward; for all the land which thou seest, to thee will I give it." (Genesis 13:14, 15)

After Jehovah instructed him to picture the good he wanted, Abraham moved his tents to the Plain of Mamre in the Land of Hebron. From this episode, you learn an invaluable success secret: Abraham did not sulk when Lot took the rich land. Abraham let him have it, and then started picturing his own increased holdings in all directions.

But he went further: He moved into the Land of Hebron which symbolizes "concentration on abundant ideas." *Spasmodically picturing your good is not enough.* In order to produce worthwhile results you, too, must concentrate on abundant ideas. This is the secret of demonstrating increased supply! ("Mamre" means "abundantly supplied.")

How A Divorcee And Her Family Prospered Through Picturing

A divorcee, who had suffered financial lack most of her life, learned of the prospering power of pictures. She made a Prosperity Map for herself and her family. On it she placed pictures of her daughters, with play money around them. She pictured a whole new life for herself.

One daughter was soon given a scholarship to cover most of her college education. A part time job provided the balance. The other daughter married well and became financially secure. The divorced mother moved out of town into one of the richest resort communities in the country, where she built a whole new prosperous life style for herself, surrounded by wealth and beauty. It all began with pictures.

How Picturing Prospered An Insurance Executive

Instead of fighting financial limitation in your life, you can picture your way out of it! The President of an insurance company recently related at one of my Mid-West seminars how picturing had prospered him, in spite of recession.

Early in his career, he made a success graph on which he pictured the financial progress he wanted his new company to make, annually, for the next 10 years. In spite of "inflationary recession" his company is one year ahead of the financial success pictured on that chart! When he displayed his success graph at the seminar, it was impressive. This executive proved that *you can picture a thing and bring it through rather than trying to reason it through or force it through. You can hasten your good through picturing it!*

As Abraham discovered, you can mold the substance of
the universe into definite, tangible results through picturing
what you want. Generalities do not produce results, because
they lack substance and power. Vague hopes and indefi-
nite goals are not convincing to the mind. But a clear-cut
picture of the good you want activates people, places, and
events to cooperate with your pictured desires.

How Realtor Raised Money For An Investment

A man in the real estate business wanted to buy an apartment house that was for sale, but he had been unable to
raise the money. Even though financing had not been arranged, he spent some time every day in quiet meditation,
picturing himself as the owner of that building. When he
gained a sense of peace about the matter, he released it from
his mind.

While negotiating a loan on other properties one day,
one of his millionaire-benefactors learned of his desire to
own the apartment house and quickly arranged financing.
But nothing happened until the realtor had first pictured it!

To remind yourself of the fantastic power of pictures
declare often: "I PICTURE MY GOOD AND BRING IT
THROUGH RATHER THAN TRYING TO REASON
IT THROUGH OR FORCE IT THROUGH. I HASTEN
MY GOOD THROUGH PICTURING IT." (Instructions
for making a Prosperity Map are found at the conclusion
of Chapter 7.)

How To Protect Your Prosperity

In the Land of Hebron, Abraham sealed or protected
his prosperity by doing something the ancient people often

did when their prayers had been answered: He built an altar to God.

When the Hebrews built altars and gave sacrifices, these acts carried financial significance. It meant that they made financial offerings to Jehovah.

They often built altars and gave "faith offerings" *before* their prayers were answered. They often built altars and gave "thank offerings" *after* their prayers had been answered, in appreciation. They felt that giving *before* a prayer was answered opened the way to receive that answer. They felt that the act of giving *after* answered prayer helped seal or protect the result and make it permanent.

Abraham's giving at this point indicated his thanks that the good he was picturing had and would come in ever increasing degrees. His gift was both a "faith offering" and a "thank offering."

This age-old prosperity technique still works for those who use it. A woman of wealth said, "When anything negative happens to me, I know it is an indication that I have not been giving enough. I always get busy and give either a 'faith offering' or a 'thank offering' to protect my wealth. This method has always prospered and protected me."

How To Be Lavishly Prospered

When Lot got involved with the enemy forces who occupied the Plain of Jordan, Abraham graciously rescued him. (Lot symbolizes the negative side of faith that judges according to appearances and has to learn that things are usually not what they seem.)

Upon returning home from victory in battle, Abraham tithed a tenth of the vast wealth gathered in battle. He gave this fortune to the High Priest of Salem. In return the Priest blessed him, and Jehovah made Abraham a promise that carries vast financial significance for us today: "Fear not, I am thy shield and thy exceeding great reward." (Genesis 15:1)

Although the act of tithing was an ancient prosperity practice, many of our modern millionaires attribute their lavish wealth to this practice. Why? Because giving is good, but consistent giving through the act of tithing one-tenth of all one receives to God's work is far better. Consistent giving opens the way to consistent receiving. As promised Abraham, those who tithe are not only prospered exceedingly, even lavishly, but they are also protected from the negative experiences of life. Vast wealth always brings the need for protection. Tithing gives that assurance.

You can be consistently prospered despite "recessional-inflation" when you practice consistent giving through the act of tithing. In the process you should claim for yourself the same millionaire promise that was made to Abraham: "I FEAR NOT, BECAUSE GOD IS MY SHIELD, AND MY EXCEEDING GREAT REWARD." (The mystical millionaire to whom Abraham tithed such lavish wealth will be discussed in Chapter 3.)

How He Went From $1000 Annually to $100,000 Annually

A young businessman, with a growing family to support, heard of this mystic law of prosperity and began to practice tithing of his income at a time when he was making only $1000 a year. Of course, he was barely surviving financially.

He tithed anyway—as an act of faith. Since faith moves on substance, his faithful tithing helped him gradually to prosper. Within 10 years, he was making $10,000 a year. (It seemed a fortune at the time.) Then he began to tithe 2/10's of his income. Within another 10 years, his income had grown to $100,000 a year! He then began to tithe 3/10's of his income.

This man recently told me that he looks forward to soon giving 5/10's—one half—of his income to God's work (Internal Revenue now allows up to 5/10's of one's income to be given as a religious and charitable deduction.) He now lives in lavish surroundings and enjoys the company of those of vast wealth. His giving has made him rich, and his gifts have vastly prospered the church that taught him the prospering power of tithing!

The Hebrew's Secret Name For Prosperity

Later Abraham attempted to sacrifice his son, Isaac, thinking that he should do so. Jehovah pointed out that such an act was not necessary, and Abraham immediately named the place of intended sacrifice "Jehovah-jireh," declaring jubilantly "In the mount of Jehovah it shall be provided." (Genesis 22:14)

"Jehovah-jireh" was the Hebrews' mystical name for prosperity. It meant "The Lord will provide for you, regardless of opposing circumstances." When financial limitation is staring you in the face, use it!

How They Went From Rags To Riches

During the Depression years of the 1930's, a businessman could not get work. His wife heard of the prospering power that can be released through declaring that secret name for prosperity, "JEHOVAH-JIREH." She began to spend a few minutes each day privately declaring, "JE-HOVAH-JIREH, THE LORD (LAW) RICHLY PROVIDES FOR US NOW." Her husband soon got a job. It was not one that measured up to his fine executive abilities, but it put food on the table.

Realizing the prospering power in that Sacred Name, this man began joining his wife each night in declaring, "JE-HOVAH-JIREH, THE LORD RICHLY PROVIDES FOR US NOW." He was soon offered a better job. As they continued to call on this Name daily, he got work in line with his fine training and executive ability. Over the years he continued to get one promotion after another with this large corporation. Finally he became one of its highest paid executives!

This man never let his success "go to his head" but continued to join his wife daily in affirming and meditating upon that sacred name, "JEHOVAH-JIREH." Together they traveled the world for his company on a generous expense allowance. After his death, his wife was provided a handsome pension. She felt the mystic power in that Name had led them from rags to riches.

A Millionaire Promise For You

Along with the other prosperity methods Abraham used to become the Bible's first historical millionaire, he employed a basic prosperity principle you can use often. He constantly asked Jehovah for guidance and he received it. Abraham proved the prospering power of that statement: "I DO NOT DEPEND UPON PERSONS OR CONDITIONS FOR MY PROSPERITY. GOD IS THE SOURCE OF MY SUPPLY, AND GOD PROVIDES

HIS OWN AMAZING CHANNELS OF PROSPERITY
TO ME NOW."

In return for his faith, Jehovah made Abraham promises
of the unlimited good that would come to his heirs. They
included vast wealth, many heirs, a longed-for Promised
Land for his descendants. (Genesis 22:17, 18) From Abraham we learn patience, because it was to be many years before all of these promises would be fulfilled for his kinsmen.
But he taught them to believe as they waited and grew into
their expanded good. He proved the prospering power of
faith.

The Bible summed up his success: "Jehovah had blessed
Abraham in all ways." (Genesis 24:1) This millionaire
promise applies to you, too, as you follow Abraham's example in invoking the prospering power of faith through
the use of "the dynamic laws of prosperity"—which include
his use of release, forming a vacuum, forgiveness, picturing, prosperity affirmations, tithing, giving "thank offerings"
and "faith offerings," and through claiming your heritage
of wealth on all levels of life.

You can get busy helping your dreams come true by de-
claring daily, "I HAVE FAITH IN GOD. I HAVE FAITH
IN PEOPLE. I HAVE FAITH IN THINGS." This is how
Abraham became a millionaire.

SUMMARY

1. Adam, the Bible's allegorical millionaire, misused his mind powers to dwell on the belief in lack, and fell from his heritage of abundance. Adam symbolizes every man who has done this.

2. Abraham, the Bible's first historical millionaire, shows us how to reclaim our heritage of lavish abundance through some simple acts of faith.

3. Abraham's life in Babylon gave him both a material and spiritual understanding of prosperity. Abraham symbolizes the man of faith who goes from a competitive sweat-of-the-brow understanding of prosperity to a creative understanding of prosperity which is invoked through the action of the mind.

4. The Land of Canaan into which Abraham went symbolizes "realm of substance." Our acts of faith move on substance and form it as rich results in our lives.

5. The acts of faith which Abraham performed were these:

    (a) He left his old country of Babylon and went into the Land of Canaan. This symbolizes releasing old possessions, relationships, and ways of living for new and better ones. It includes the practice of forgiveness and making an elimination list.

    (b) When Lot took the richest land from him, Abraham looked up and pictured the good in all directions and became very rich. You can picture your way out of limitation. Make a success map.

    (c) He practiced giving through "faith offerings" and "thank offerings" by building an altar to God and giving financial sacrifices. We should too.

(d) He tithed "a tenth of all" to the High Priest of Salem. Tithing is the mystic law of prosperity because consistent giving opens the way to consistent receiving.

(e) "Jehovah-jireh" was the sacred Hebrew name for prosperity. It releases prosperity to those who affirm that name.

6. Abraham's basic prosperity secret was that he constantly asked Jehovah for guidance and got it. He did not depend upon persons or conditions.

7. In return for Abraham's faith, Jehovah blessed him in all ways and promised lavish abundance for his descendants as well.

8. As we use the simple prosperity methods Abraham used, our faith moves on the rich substance of the universe and opens the way for our heritage of lavish abundance to manifest.

THE MYSTICAL MILLIONAIRE--
MELCHIZEDEK

HIS PROSPERITY SECRETS FOR YOU

— Chapter 3 —

It is in the life of Abraham that you meet the mystical millionaire, Melchizedek, who was both King of Salem and its High Priest. He is a mysterious figure in the Old Testament because nothing is definitely known of his background. It is believed that he was a descendant of one of the Babylonian high priests and probably distant kin of Abraham.

According to ancient legend, Melchizedek conducted a Wisdom School in Babylon which Abraham attended during that first period of his life when Abraham lived in Babylon. You can learn certain prosperity principles from the elegant Melchizedek that are indispensible to a permanent, enduring wealth.

56

How Your Prosperity Can Become An Automatic Process

There are many success courses and self-help books on the subject of prosperity available today, and they are all good. Any instruction that helps you to open your mind to increased abundance is worthwhile. But most of those courses —which often cost hundreds of dollars—and many of the success books—cover only a fraction of the prosperity principles practiced by the millionaires of Genesis, as reported in this book.

Most of the success courses and books available today explain how you can create your prosperity mentally first through deciding what you want and then going after it through the goal-setting methods of: 1) Writing it down. 2) Picturing it. 3) Affirming it. Those prosperity techniques are very good. As will be shown in this book, the millionaires of Genesis used them.

But unless you: 1) Realize that prosperity is your spiritual heritage and then cleanse your mind of guilt about wanting to be prospered; 2) Learn how to get out of the "old country" by forgiving, releasing, and giving up limited states of mind and circumstances that you have outgrown, as did Abraham; 3) Give your prosperity a spiritual basis as did Abraham when he tithed to Melchizedek—your prosperity may not be permanent.

Through use of the strictly mental laws of prosperity, you may be able to excite temporary results. But you will sink down into frustrated despair later when those temporary results fade away. (I have talked with many people who have had this experience.)

By learning the *entire* formula for prosperity—including the advanced law of prosperity as taught by the mystical millionaire, Melchizedek — and as practiced by the millionaire Abraham—you will find that your prosperity becomes an automatic process. There will be nothing "hit or miss" about it. You will enjoy demonstrating permanent, enduring prosperity without experiencing the strained frustration of those still working at it from the competitive, hardwork, take-all, give-nothing level.

How To Overcome Lawsuits, Bankruptcy, and Other Severe Financial Problems

This was brought to my attention at a prosperity seminar I conducted in San Antonio, Texas, which was attended by business and professional people from all over the United States and Canada. In attendance were several millionaires, at least a dozen Army and Air Force officers, one surgeon, several doctors of chiropractic, a dentist, a professor of economics, the owner of a chain of health spas, several ministers including the famous "Reverend Ike" of New York City, secretaries, housewives, a judge, and business people in general.

The day after the seminar concluded, a number of those who had attended stopped by my office (which was then located in San Antonio) for a quick visit on their way to the airport. Their reaction to their review of the laws of prosperity was much the same.

Over and over in private conversation they said: "I have taken many business and professional success courses, for which I paid hundreds, sometimes thousands, of dollars. But none of them taught me the greatest prosperity law of all—that of tithing. Those success courses gave me a lift at the time I took them, but later I felt let down and frustrated because they did not seem to work on a permanent basis. Now I know why. None of those courses pointed out that my prosperity must have a spiritual basis in order to last. I am relieved to know that tithing hastens and stabilizes one's success. I am going home to tithe my way to prosperity."

One man had several lawsuits pending against him. Another was facing bankruptcy. Both vowed to tithe their way out of these financial problems into wealth and affluence again.

Meet The Mystical Millionaire Within You

Melchizedek held great fascination for both Jewish and Christian writers because he was the mystical millionaire to whom Abraham gave a fortune in tithes. He holds great fascination for us today because this wealthy King of Salem and High Priest symbolizes that mystical millionaire that resides within everyone of us—including you—known as "Jehovah," "I AM," or "The Christ Mind."

Melchizedek symbolizes the third level of the mind that resides within all men, but of which only a few illumined ones are aware. This is the miracle level of the mind which, when activated, can produce prosperous results in your life quickly. People in all ages have known about this third level of the mind, which they often described as the "superconscious." But rarely have they realized that within their superconsciousness was a mystical millionaire whose power could be activated for their increased prosperity!

Early Psychologists Knew About This Mystical Millionaire

Two noted psychologists were the Swiss doctor Carl Jung and the father of American psychology, William James. Both felt that man has not only a conscious mind with which he daily thinks, and a subconscious mind which contains his memory and emotions, but that man also has a deeper third phase of the mind—a superconscious level—in which resides an Infinite Intelligence that longs to work for and through both the conscious and subconscious phases of the mind to produce fantastic good in man's life quickly.

What these psychologists referred to as Superconsciousness, Divine Intelligence, Divine Mind, or the "I AM" power in man, is sometimes called "The Christ Mind," or "the Christ Consciousness." (Probably this is because Jesus Christ seemed to have developed perfectly this miracle level of the mind. This is reflected in His ability to manifest instant loaves, fishes, wine, and tax money. It was also from this miracle level of the mind that He healed the multitudes and even raised some persons from the dead.)

How to Activate This Mystical Millionaire

The ancient people had various secret names they intoned for activating this Superconsciousness. They knew that this third level of the mind is filled with miracle power.

They felt that if you would hold to that secret word, motto, or text in time of trial, it would rearrange your affairs and bring you through to victory. The people of the Old Testament did this by dwelling upon the sacred names "I AM" and "JEHOVAH." The early Christians did so by dwelling upon the names "JESUS CHRIST" and "CHRIST JESUS."

How They Activated Great Wealth With This Method

A sickly, poverty-stricken young man learned of the mystical millionaire within him and began to activate it by calling upon the Name "I AM" in his daily meditations. First came health. Gradually came vast wealth as he continued to call on this mystical Name for prosperity.

A divorced woman was heartbroken over the years she had given to her tyrant-husband. In order to save her sanity and recover her health, she finally divorced him. Her life seemed in shambles until she learned of the mystical millionaire within her.

As she, too, began to call daily on the Name "I AM" in meditation, *first* her health improved; *second* she got work she enjoyed; *third* she met and married into one of America's super-rich families. She continues to enjoy the countless benefits that vast wealth brings.

Why You Are Master of Substance and Vast Wealth

You can make contact with this mystical millionaire in the miracle level of your mind in several ways, and reap prosperous results.

It is significant that this mystical millionaire was King of Salem because "Salem" means "a place of peace, prosperity, wholeness, and perfection." Salem was later called Jerusalem, which means "realm of substance." As the ruler of Jerusalem, King Melchizedek was master of that realm of substance which is the basis of all wealth, and so are you!

Since every person has this mystical millionaire within him, you can become master of substance and manifest it as peace, prosperity, wholeness, and perfection in your life. You can begin activating this mystical millonaire which resides in the I AM or Christ Mind within you by meditating often upon this statement: "I AM MASTER OF DIVINE SUBSTANCE. I AM. I AM. I AM. I CLAIM MY MASTERY OF DIVINE SUBSTANCE NOW. DIVINE SUBSTANCE NOW MANIFESTS FOR ME AS PEACE, WHOLENESS, PROSPERITY, PERFECTION."

How The Mystical Millionaire Can Prosper You

When Abraham returned from doing battle with Lot's adversaries, he was met by King Melchizedek, who gave him bread and wine. Then the King blessed him.

That mystical millionaire within you, the rich I AM or Christ Mind, is constantly pouring out upon you bread and wine—often in the form of rich ideas and opportunities. That same rich I AM, or Infinite Intelligence, is constantly blessing you, just as this elegant King blessed Abraham. But usually you have not received the intended gifts, nor have you received the lavish blessing accompanying them.

You can receive the wealth of the universe which that mystical millionaire is constantly trying to pour out upon you in the following simple ways:

1) By realizing that it is spiritually right, instead of spiritually wrong, for you to be prospered. 2) By feeling elated rather than guilty about wanting to prosper. 3) By realizing that prosperity is a necessity because it gives you freedom from bondage to people, places, or possessions. 4) By realizing that it gives you freedom to grow, and to expand your world in countless ways.

You can receive the wealth of the universe, which that mystical millionaire is trying to pour out upon you, by opening your mind to it. Declare often, "I NOW OPEN MY MIND TO RICH IDEAS, AND TO RICH RESULTS. I AM RICH IN MIND AND IN MANIFESTATION NOW."

You can begin to receive the wealth of the universe which that mystical millionaire has for you by speaking the word of receiving. Say often, "I AM RECEIVING. I AM RECEIVING NOW. I AM RECEIVING ALL THE WEALTH THAT THE UNIVERSE HAS FOR ME NOW."

How To Multiply Money

Not only did Melchizedek give Abraham bread and wine, but he also blessed him. You have access to that same rich blessing too!

A blessing is always an invaluable gift. Whatever is blessed increases. Blessing substance increases its flow. If your money is low or your purse empty, take it in your hands and bless it. See it filled with Divine Substance, manifesting for you as money, money, money. Declare "I BLESS ALL THAT I HAVE AND I LOOK WITH WONDER AT ITS INCREASE NOW."

When preparing meals, bless the food knowing it is Divine Substance. When you dress, bless your garments as Divine Substance. Realize that you are constantly being clothed with the rich substance of the universe. The more you recognize and bless Divine Substance, the more it will manifest for you, and the richer you will become.

Declare often, "I BLESS MY WORLD WITH PEACE, PROSPERITY, WHOLENESS, AND PERFECTION NOW." Such words carry the wealthy blessing that the mystical millionaire gave to Abraham—that man of faith—so many centuries ago. That same blessing is meant for all who have the faith to claim it today, including you!

A Formula That Can Prosper You Mightily

Abraham made contact with the lavish flow of substance offered him by the King of Salem by performing an act of faith. He knew that faith moves on substance, and that his acts of faith would help him to keep in touch with the unlimited substance that Melchizedek was offering him.

Abraham's act of faith was to tithe "a tenth of all" (Genesis 14:20) the fortune he had collected in battle to this wealthy High Priest. In this simple act, you find a formula that can prosper you mightily!

The great temples of Babylon were lavishly supported by the tithes levied upon prince and peasant alike. In his Babylonian home, Abraham had become familiar with the practice of tithing. He knew that *the consistent practice of tithing had made the Babylonians one of the richest nations of ancient times.*

Since ancient times it has been proved that those who tithe 10 percent of their income to God's work find that their prosperity increases by leaps and bounds, until all fear of poverty has disappeared. The act of tithing gives your prosperity a permanent, enduring basis. *To practice tithing is a fascinating and mystical way to be prospered.*

The ancient people felt that "ten" was "the magic number of increase" which they invoked through their systematic tithes. They knew the word "tithe" means "tenth."

How His Second Million Came More Easily

It is common knowledge that many of the most successful businessmen of the present day—great industrialists and captains of industry — attribute their success to having formed the habit of tithing. *Hundreds of thousands of people have grown out of poverty into financial affluence and comfort through the practice of tithing. Hundreds of thousands more are doing so today!*

A young tycoon attended one of my prosperity seminars. At the close he said, "I made my first million through sweat-of-the-brow methods. It was hard work and I always feared losing it. Now I see why it was such a strain. I did not invoke the mystical law of tithing, which would give my wealth protection and permanence. I now plan to tithe my way into my second million, and I expect it to be much easier to make and to keep this time."

A Businessman's Million-Dollar Formula

You can see how consistent giving to God's work opens the way to consistent receiving in your own work. It is a practice that is businesslike, orderly, scientific, and practical. If the farmer refused to give back to the soil a certain percentage of the crops which the soil had given to him, he would have no crops.

Since God is the Source of your supply, you must do something definite and consistent to keep in touch with that rich Source, if you want to be consistently prospered. Those who tithe are always certain they will prosper because they have the confidence and faith that goes with having God as a partner.

Life-long poverty has been overcome through the practice of tithing. (I can personally attest to that!) One businessman who went from rags to riches, after a lifetime of poverty, explained it simply: "I tithed my way to prosperity." It was his million-dollar formula.

Throughout Hebrew history, they gave not the last and the least, but the first and the best. And their giving made them rich!

Why Her Prosperity Stopped

The act of giving restores a harmony and balance in both mind and body that results in happiness as well as prosperity. When your life gets out of harmony, you need to give in order to restore balance and abundance.

A businesswoman learned that the act of giving restores balance and harmony, which results in both happiness and prosperity. She began consistently to tithe to the church where she had learned this prosperity secret. It worked. She was prospered in her business. Then she was offered a business opportunity that could make her a millionaire. She took the new job, but was so confident of prospering that she no longer tithed.

One day she said to a friend, "I cannot understand it. I was guided to accept this business opportunity, but nothing is working out right."

The friend suggested that she review the laws of prosperity to discover which ones she was no longer using. When she did, she quickly realized she had stopped tithing. At this point she had only $500 left in her checking account for both living and business expenses. She boldly wrote out a tithe for $50 and put it in the mail to her church. Customers soon appeared for her new business, things straightened out in other phases of her life, and she has prospered again. *Money invested in spiritual things is never loss but gain a hundredfold!*

How She Paid Off $9000 Indebtedness

Perhaps you are thinking, "But I cannot afford to tithe." That is when you cannot afford *not* to tithe! The greater the present financial necessity, the greater the need for invoking "ten, the magic number of increase."

You can tithe your way out of indebtedness! A businessman, who had always felt he could not afford to tithe, found himself $9000 in debt at the time of his retirement. However, his wife had been a lifelong tither of her own income. Upon his retirement, she took over their financial affairs. Within 2 years she had paid off $7000 of her husband's longstanding debt of $9000! Soon thereafter she paid off the balance. She proved that *tithing is the beginning of permanent financial increase.*

How A Housewife Came Into A Large Inheritance

One housewife has often restored balance in her financial affairs by tithing in advance. When she has a financial need, she gives a tithe of the amount she hopes to receive in *advance*. For instance, if she hopes to receive $500 she gives an advance tithe of $50. It is little wonder she recently became the recipient of a large inheritance!

Even though the rich I AM or Christ Mind, which King Melchizedek symbolizes, is constantly offering you unlimited supply, you have to do something as an act of faith to make contact with that lavish abundance. Your acts of faith move on substance and manifest it as rich supply—as this housewife proved.

Where You Give Is Important

"People are down on what they are not up on." People have sometimes had a psychological block against tithing, because well-meaning theologians have often stressed what tithing would do for the church, rather than what it would do for the individual.

The act of tithing, or giving back to God's work one-tenth of your gross income ("a tenth of all" Genesis 14:20), is not something that some minister dreamed up as a means of getting money out of you! It is a universal prosperity law that has been practiced since the beginning of time as a scientific and orderly method of prospering people on a permanent basis.

When you look up the great tithing promises in the Bible, such as the one given by the prophet Malachi (Malachi 3:10), you find that the illumined of Bible times promised that the individual who tithes will be prospered. Of course, his church will be prospered too. But that is the secondary, not the primary cause for tithing. As *you* tithe, so *you* prosper is the promise. Protection is also assured the tither: "Bring ye the whole tithe into the storehouse, that there may be food in my house, and prove me now herewith, saith Jehovah of hosts, if I will not open you the windows of heaven, and pour you out a blessing, that there shall not be room enough to receive it." (PROSPERITY PROMISE) "And I will rebuke the devourer for your sakes, and he shall not destroy the fruits of your ground; neither shall your vine cast its fruit before the time in the field." (PROMISE OF PROTECTION) (Malachi 3:10, 11)

Be careful *where* you give your tithe. It is important that you give at the point or points where you are receiving spiritual help and inspiration.

A businesswoman once said, "I have some apartments that I cannot keep rented, although I use all the prosperity laws. And don't tell me to tithe because I'm also doing that."

"Where are you tithing?"

"I cannot see that it matters where I tithe, so I give my tithes to the church I used to attend, because they keep billing me. But I now attend another church where I get far more inspiration."

The answer was, "Tithe where you are getting help and inspiration if you wish to be prospered. It is inconsistent to do otherwise. To get inspirational help from one church, yet tithe to another is like going to one doctor for help, yet trying to pay another; or like eating in one restaurant, yet paying for your meal in another restaurant. Give at the point or points where you are receiving spiritual help and inspiration. This keeps you in touch with the flow of supply."

How Wrong Distribution of Tithes Caused
Financial Problems

People sometimes say, "It is difficult to know where to give my tithes, because there are so many 'needy' causes that are crying out for support."

True. But there is a standard rule that will guide you rightly in your giving—one laid down in ancient times—as a businessman discovered. This man was in the real estate business and got careless with the distribution of his tithes.

One month he gave his tithes to a problem-prone relative, rather than giving it impersonally to his church. Everything went wrong. His bank account got mixed up and a number of checks bounced. A real estate deal, from which he expected a commission of several thousand dollars, did not go through. Other channels of supply dried up and he was left in a financial bind.

Everything stagnated until he put God—and not a problem-prone relative—first again financially. There is nothing wrong in helping one in need, if you are careful *what* you give. By giving them only money, you offer only temporary help. Your charity can even keep them in poverty. It is far wiser to give them books and literature that show them how to use the laws of prosperity for themselves. This will help those in need to become self-supporting, even permanently prosperous. It will help them to become independent of poverty programs or charity hand-outs.

The Ancient Law On Where To Give

The ancient laws on tithing were very definite about where the tithe was to be given. The first tenth went to the priests, who then gave a tenth of that tithe, known as a "heave offering," to the place of worship. This first tithe was given impersonally. The giver had nothing to say about how it was to be spent. The second tithe was a festival tithe, and the third tithe was for charity. (Numbers 18:26)

If you are giving several tenths of your income rather than only one tenth, then you should feel freer with your second or third tithe. But your first tithe should be given impersonally to God's work—or to individuals in spiritual work who have inspired you—with no stipulation of how it is to be spent by the recipient. (Nehemiah 10:38)

It is interesting to note that under Mosaic law, the people of the Old Testament gave away 4/10's of their income—three tithes plus "first fruits" of all their crops—yet they never complained about giving too much. Instead, the more they gave, the wealthier they became. They suffered financial reverses only when they became self-satisfied and stopped tithing during the latter part of Solomon's reign. Then came financial disaster and exile.

When They Held Back, It Was Withheld From Them

You learn of this mystic law of prosperity when you are ready in your expanded understanding to begin using it. You soon discover that if you do not give voluntarily to the constructive experiences of life, you will find yourself giving involuntarily to the destructive experiences of life—but give you must. It is the law of the universe.

Several friends were working together on a special project that lasted a week. Every night after work on this project, they would go out together to eat. Three of these people took turns paying for the evening meals. The fourth one did not offer to pay for anything.

After concluding this special work project, on their last night together, they decided to dine out in special celebration. Again the fourth member of the group paid for nothing, though she enjoyed a lavish meal in beautiful surroundings. On the way home that night, she discovered that she had lost about $50 in cash. Some prized jewelry she had been wearing was also missing. She had quickly proved the law: *Hold back and it will be withheld, even taken, from you.*

How Tithing Brings Job

A businessman heard of this mystic law of giving and wrote out a check for $60 to his church at a time when he was in financial straits. His giving enriched him. He got the finest job of his life!

Why The Hebrew Priests Were Millionaires

That Melchizedek was not only a King but a priest of great wealth has prosperous significance. In ancient times the priests were millionaires because the people gave their tithes to the priests, who then gave a "tithe of the tithe" to the place of worship. Wealth was considered a necessity for the priesthood because it freed those in spiritual work from financial burdens and strain. Their wealth freed them to devote their time to the development of their own spirituality and that of their followers. (Melchizedek's tithes from the spoils of war were worth a fortune.)

Also the people of ancient times felt they should give to a consciousness of prosperity rather than to a consciousness of lack and need, if they wished to continue in their own prosperity. They knew that "nothing succeeds like success" and "For whosoever hath, to him shall be given and he shall have abundance; but whosoever hath not, from him shall be taken away even that which he hath." (Matthew 13:12) They felt it was necessary for their priests and spiritual leaders to be lavishly prospered, that they might continue sharing a prosperity consciousness with their followers.

Freedom from material care is still essential to the development of your deeper powers. Keeping the law of giving and receiving is still recognized as a great step in your spiritual development.

Do Not Apologize When You Become A Millionaire

As you use the mystical law of tithing, do not apologize for the prosperity and success that begins to flow to you. Do not apologize even when you become a millionaire! There are enough riches available to make every person a millionaire without injury to another. There are enough prosperity laws available for man's use to make every person a millionaire, without depleting anyone else.

Of course, there is also a plentiful supply of poverty for those who ignorantly want it. Those who ignore the inner laws of prosperity that were used by the millionaires of Genesis will continue to reap a harvest of limitation. However, as you use the mystical law of prosperity—as described in this chapter—you will surely reap its rich benefits.

For this purpose declare often: "I NO LONGER STRAIN AND STRIVE. I TITHE AND THRIVE. AS I FREELY GIVE MY TENTH TO GOD, I REAP A HUNDREDFOLD INCREASE."

A SPECIAL NOTE FROM THE AUTHOR

"Through the generous outpouring of their tithes over the years, the readers of my books have helped me to financially establish 3 new churches—the most recent being a global ministry, *Unity Church Worldwide*, with headquarters in Palm Desert, California. Many thanks for your help in the past, and for all that you continue to share.

"You are also invited to share your tithes with the churches of your choice—especially those which teach the truths stressed in this book. Such churches would include the metaphysical churches of Unity, Religious Science, Divine Science, Science of Mind and other related churches, many of which are members of the International New Thought Movement. (For a list of such churches write The International New Thought Alliance, 7314 East Stetson Drive, Scottsdale, Arizona 85251.) Your support of such churches can help spread the prosperous Truth that mankind is now seeking in the New Age of metaphysical enlightenment."

SUMMARY

1. Melchizedek was the mystical millionaire to whom Abraham gave a fortune in tithes. Melchizedek symbolizes that mystical millionaire that resides within each of us, known as "the Christ Mind or "I AM."

2. Melchizedek was King of Salem. The word "Salem" means "a place of peace, prosperity, wholeness and perfection." Salem was later called Jerusalem which means "realm of substance." As the ruler of Jerusalem, King Melchizedek was master of that realm of substance.

3. Since every man has this mystical millionaire (the Christ Mind) within him, every man can become master of substance and manifest it as peace, prosperity, wholeness and perfection in his life.

4. The mystical millionaire within us is constantly pouring out upon us bread and wine or the rich substance of the universe, as did Melchizedek through his gifts to Abraham.

5. That mystical millionaire within us is constantly trying to bless us, just as King Melchizedek blessed Abraham.

6. You can open your mind to receive the wealth of the universe which the mystical millionaire is pouring out upon you by opening your mind to rich ideas and rich results. Also by speaking the word of receiving.

7. You have access to that same rich power of blessing as did Abraham. Bless all that you have and look with wonder at its increase. What you bless multiplies.

8. Abraham made contact with the lavish flow of substance offered by the King of Salem by performing an act of faith. He knew that faith moves on substance.

9. Abraham's act of faith was to tithe a tenth of the fortune he had collected in battle to this priest. He knew that "ten" was "the magic number of increase."

10. Hundreds of thousands of people have grown out of poverty into financial affluence and comfort through the practice of tithing. Your giving can make you rich. As you tithe so you prosper.

11. Consistent giving restores balance in both mind and body that results in happiness as well as prosperity.

12. As you tithe and prosper, do not apologize for your success. Wealth is your heritage.

THE PEACEFUL MILLIONAIRE--
ISAAC

HIS PROSPERITY SECRETS FOR YOU

— Chapter 4 —

From the millionaire, Isaac, you learn how to increase your income a hundredfold in just one year!

Isaac has been described as "the man of peace." He was so peaceful that his importance has often been overlooked. Isaac has been regarded only as the rich son of Abraham— a quiet, pleasant man, but unassertive. Historians have described him as a gentleman. Abraham raised his son in the cultured, refined ways of the Babylonians. History reveals that Rebekah married Isaac for his money. She knew he was a millionaire and the son of a millionaire.

From a financial standpoint, there seemed little reason for Isaac to work. He was well provided for by his father, who finally gave him a fortune. (Genesis 25:5) But in spite of wealthy surroundings and a rich inheritance, Isaac *did* work. He demonstrated prosperity on his own in a big way: "Isaac sowed in the land and the same year reaped a hundredfold." (Genesis 26:12)

The lavish abundance that came to him from his own efforts, independent of the vast wealth which Abraham bestowed upon him, has been described: "And Jehovah blessed him, and he waxed great, and grew more and more until he became very great; and he had possessions of flocks, and possessions of herds, and a great household." (Genesis 26:12-14)

The Prospering Power of Joy

How did this quiet, pleasant, unassertive man increase his income a hundredfold in just one year? The clue to his success is found in his name. The word "Isaac" means "joy, laughter, happiness, peace." Just as Isaac was a well opener, the power of joy opens up many powers deep within man's being, and releases them as great good in his life.

The pleasant state of mind is an attracting power for prosperity and success; whereas the unpleasant, overserious, strained, overworked state of mind repels prosperity. This explains why some people work hard all their lives, yet are never prospered. They are too serious, and radiate a strained vibration that repels prosperity.

There is a mystical saying that explains: "Has a joyous declaration been recurring all the way through your life? If not, you have had a great deal of defeat you were not entitled to."

There once was a lady who felt she could not go on. In mourning over the death of her husband, she was heavily in debt and both mentally and physically exhausted.

One night when she was struggling mentally just to survive, she heard the word "joy" as though someone had spoken it to her. Her first reaction was, "What do I have to be joyous about?" The thought came, "At least you have the gift of life." Other blessings came to mind: Friends, family, job.

She began to say, "JOY, JOY, JOY. MY LIFE IS NOW FILLED WITH JOY." Things began to improve at once. Her grief slowly healed. Members of her family obtained jobs. A relative recovered from a grave illness. Her own work became easier and she began to clear away her indebtedness. In time joy had overcome all of her problems.

The Prospering Power of Peace

The peaceful state of mind, which Isaac symbolizes, has been underestimated. A healing method that became famous early in this century was very simple: The metaphysician who developed it got people into a relaxed, peaceful state of mind. Healing occurred naturally.

In the word "peace" is found every element of good: Life, love, wisdom, power, substance. The mystics have long taught that the consciousness of peace is always the forerunner of victory. *In the peaceful state of mind are found all of the blessings of life.* The peaceful state of mind will win out against all odds. It will always demonstrate good results for you. Isaac proved this with the Philistines in his "wells of abundance" experiences—as related later in this chapter.

You can gain control of your mind, body, financial affairs, and relationships with others by first speaking words of "peace."

The Psalmist knew that peace and prosperity are related when he affirmed, "Peace be within thy walls, and prosperity within thy palaces." (Psalms 122:7) Isaac proved that peace and prosperity go hand in hand. He increased his income a hundredfold in one year through a peaceful state of mind that was coupled with outer action as a farmer.

The Prospering Power of Beauty

Isaac's wife, Rebekah, symbolizes "the soul's natural delight in beauty." When Abraham's servant approached her at the well for the first time, he made her acquaintance by giving her gifts of jewelry as a token of wealth from his rich master, Abraham, who was seeking a wife for Isaac. Rebekah was delighted with the jewelry and the vast wealth it represented.

As you begin to think along prosperous lines, you will become more sensitive to beauty. Beauty will give you a sense of peace and satisfaction that nothing else can. It will feed your inner nature. This is why you will crave more beauty in your world.

When your are trying to demonstrate increased prosperity, "put your best foot forward." Wear your best clothes, use your best china and silver in your home. Create as much beauty as possible in your business surroundings. To do these things makes you become an attractive power for increased supply.

How A Palm Beach Apartment Came To Me

You can demonstrate prosperity by absorbing beauty. Wherever you go, absorb everything that is pleasing to your soul. Learn to drink in everything around you that you can enjoy and appreciate: Beauty, color, music, the aroma of flowers, the beautiful atmosphere of a room, building, or out-of-doors. This feeds your inner nature. *When your inner nature is sufficiently fed, your outer needs are far more easily met.*

I once lectured in the Palm Beach, Florida, area for a six-weeks period. Arrangements had been made for me to use a small apartment. Though it was adequate, it was not located in the "gold coast" area. Because I was lecturing on prosperity, I felt it was appropriate for me to be immersed in the millionaire consciousness of elegant Palm Beach.

Since beauty is an attracting power for prosperity, it occurred to me that I should absorb the beauty of the area. I spent an entire afternoon driving up and down the famous "County Road" that winds for miles along the Palm Beach coast line. Along with the lavish abundance of nature found in that area, there are hundreds of beautiful estates located on that route. Absorbing the beauty of that area was an unsurpassed prosperity treatment which I engaged in for several hours.

That night, following a prosperity lecture, one of my listeners sought me out and said, "I would like to express my appreciation for the help I have obtained from some of your writings. I am a Palm Beach realtor. I have a lovely furnished apartment located just a block from the ocean on

Palm Beach. It will be vacant for another six weeks. I
would like you to use it during that period—as a gift."

Within a few hours from the time I had completed my
long drive along Palm Beach, I had the key to a lovely
apartment there, which I thoroughly enjoyed for the rest of
my stay.

How I Moved Into The Most Beautiful Office Building In Town

Along with absorbing the wealth found in large areas,
another way to demonstrate prosperity is by absorbing the
wealth found in beautiful buildings. Many people do this
by visiting art galleries and studying the beauty found there.

A ministry I was once serving was in need of office space.
I felt that until we could have lovely quarters, it was best
to have none. And we did not, for some time.

Then a new building was erected in the downtown area
overlooking the State Capitol. It was by far the loveliest
building in town. I studied the advertisements which described the office space in that building, and felt it would
be ideal for our ministry to be housed there. For many
months I thought about this, but it seemed a preposterous
idea financially.

When the desire persisted, I realized that was a divine
indication that I should do something to mentally accept
that possibility. On the first floor of that new building was
a lovely beauty salon. The Governor's wife was a regular
customer. I began using that salon weekly, just to get into
the elegant consciousness of that building.

Within a few months from the time I began my weekly visits to that building, a substantial offering was given the church, which made it possible for us to lease offices immediately in that building. With our offices were provided appropriate new furnishings, a fine secretary, and use of a private club at the top of the building. There we held our board meetings and other special events.

Suddenly I found myself surrounded by a consciousness of affluence. Offices on one side of ours were occupied by a retired Army general. Offices on the other side were occupied by a Texas oil man who drove to work in his Rolls Royce. Since this office building overlooked the State Capitol, the Governor and other State officials were frequent visitors in our building.

A young secretary working in a firm down the hall told me she had read some of my books. Evidence that she had came a little later when she married her wealthy and prominent boss! I continued to enjoy occupancy in that elegant building as long as I served that ministry. It was a pleasant experience.

How Isaac Manifested His "Wells of Abundance"

"A weak man fights, but a strong man governs himself to higher purposes." This statement describes how Isaac manifested his "'wells of abundance" and increased his income a hundredfold in one year. In studying the success symbology of his methods, you will find how you can increase your good a hundredfold, too!

Isaac became so wealthy that "the Philistines envied him." (Genesis 26:14) When you become more prosperous through adopting a pleasant state of mind (Isaac), and by dwelling upon beauty (Rebekah), the same thing may happen to you. If others envy you, do not be surprised and do not fight back. Hold the thought, "LOVE ENVIETH NOT. THE PROSPERING TRUTH HAS SET ME FREE TO PROSPER ABUNDANTLY."

What was the success secret of this young millionaire, who could "keep his cool" in the midst of envy, and increase his income so enormously?

Along with a quiet industriousness was coupled a success quality that is often overlooked: That of peaceful nonresistance, which the Oriental sages have often described as "divine indifference."

The dictionary describes a nonresistant person as one who refuses to use force even to defend himself. A nonresistant person is one who is neutral to and unconcerned by forceful appearances. Such nonresistance forms a vacuum, which quickly acts as a magnet to attract one's good. People often do just the opposite: They fight for their good. *The negative vibrations they stir up drive away the very good they are fighting to get!*

As a man of peace, Isaac knew that becoming inwardly still in the face of a disturbing situation was the surest way to deliverance from it. Isaac's obvious use of the success power of nonresistance is shown in the way he diplomatically handled the troublesome Philistines. This was a tribe of people against whom the Israelites were constantly trying to defend themselves.

The Philistines envied Isaac: *First,* because he was a millionaire. *Second,* because he came into their Land of Gerar and reaped a hundredfold increase in his crops there in just one short year.

In their envy of his prosperity consciousness, the Philistines asked Isaac to leave: "Go from us; thou art mightier than we." (Genesis 26:16) With his large herds, many servants, countless possessions, and vast wealth, Isaac could easily have retaliated. But he refused to fight for his rights. He released, loosed, let go, and left. He hung onto none of his valuable land.

Gerar, A Halting Place

After moving his vast possessions into the Valley of Gerar, Isaac's herdsmen began to dig wells of water. Well-digging in a land of few rivers, where rains fell only at certain seasons, was of utmost importance. However, the word "Gerar" meant "a halting place." Isaac knew this Valley of Gerar symbolized a halting place in his growth. It was not a place in which he wished to settle down.

Isaac's First and Second Wells of Abundance

Each well was given a name. From the metaphysical meaning of the name of each well, you discover how to manifest "wells of abundance" in your life too!

The first well his herdsmen dug was named "Esek" which meant "coming in touch with substance." The troublesome Philistines appeared and said, "The water is ours." (Genesis 26:20) Isaac gave them the well and moved on to another spot.

As a mystic, Isaac was doubtless aware of that age-old teaching: *Never ask why a problem has come to you, for always the indication is that your soul needs to learn the lesson to be gained in solving that problem.*

The second well was named "Sitnah" which meant "strife, contention, oppression." When the Philistines appeared and wanted these two wells, Isaac quickly released them.

He knew that in the expansion of his prosperity consciousness, he was beginning to come in touch with the inner flow of substance ("Esek"), but he did not have to settle for that limited amount. By releasing this well, he expanded into a place of greater supply.

He also knew that to have hung on to the second well would only have caused strife and contention ("Sitnah").

How These Wells of Abundance Can Have An Electrifying Effect Upon Your Life!

Can you identify with Isaac's experiences in developing his "wells of abundance?" *I* certainly can! In tracing my progress through my various life experiences — especially in my work — I find that I have been busy for a number of years digging wells of abundance in consciousness and experiencing the same outward results as did Isaac.

I can pinpoint that well-digging area in my life — Gerar — which proved to be a start in my progress, but because it was not as productive as I expected, it proved to be only a "halting place" in my growth. This motivated me to move on.

I can pinpoint my experience with that first well — "Esek" — in which I began "to come in touch with substance." It was at this point that I began to learn the deeper laws of prosperity, and to gain an understanding of the universal laws for successful living. But in my "Esek" experience I was only able to begin to become aware of them. I was not yet able to do anything more than just begin to use them step by step. It was a slow process, but one that greatly encouraged me, since I could see how this unlimited way of thinking could lead to a fabulous new way of life. The possibilities were just so exciting that they motivated me to try and try again.

I can certainly pinpoint my experience with that second well, "Sitnah." It was at that point that I began to use more fully the inner laws of success I was learning. This caused strife and contention among some unprogressive people who tried to oppress or hold me down to their limited level. That oppression was a great blessing because it prompted me to release everything gained up to that point and to move out into new experiences, where "the seals of abundance" (described in the next section) were broken in consciousness. From that point on, nothing could hold back my good! It began to flow slowly but surely, and it has been gaining momentum ever since.

The prosperity explanation of Isaac's "wells of abundance" experiences have had an electrifying effect upon so many people who have learned its deeper meaning. I trust this mystical prosperity formula will prove equally illuminating for you, too! So read on . . .

How To Break The Seals On Your Wells of Abundance

The wells his herdsmen dug symbolize an "inward source of life, a fountain of inspiration." When the "seal" is broken on this inward source of life, new substance flows forth in the form of increased energy, ideas, opportunities, and prosperous results. This leads to a renewal of the mind, body, and affairs. The "seal" is broken through continuing to dig in consciousness, or by persisting in expanding your thinking and your world.

This is exactly what Isaac did, because at this point he moved from the Valley of Gerar into his expanded good.

You can "break the seals" in consciousness on your wells of abundance through your persistent thoughts, words, and pictures of prosperity. As you get definite about prosperity in your thoughts, words, and actions, then prosperity gets definite about you, and it manifests.

How They Broke The Seals On Their Well of Abundance

A businesswoman needed more money. She began to arise before daybreak each morning and to quietly meditate upon the substance of the universe. She called it to her, until she actually felt an inner flow of energy pour forth into her world. The results? $20,000 quietly came to her in an unexpected way!

A businessman "broke the seal" in consciousness and saw his income double soon after he made a Success Map, picturing himself surrounded by money. As he privately looked at that map every day, and declared that the enormous sums of money that were his by divine right were coming to him —they did—through increased business transactions.

Isaac's Third Well of Abundance

After Isaac left the Valley of Gerar, his herdsmen dug a third well which he named "Rehoboth." It meant "a broad place, enlargement, greater expression, expansion of thought." The Philistines did not try to take this well. Instead when they appeared, they wanted to make peace with Isaac!

You may have this same experience as you expand your prosperity consciousness: When you are digging inwardly and outwardly for your good, perhaps you will get results. Yet the Philistines of limitation may appear in some form and demand the good you have realized. Like Isaac, you can know that you still have more wells to dig!

You should continue to dig deeper in consciousness because you are not yet in your true place—that big place in your growth where your full-blown good awaits you. Like Isaac, if you refuse to fight back—if you refuse to say 'My good has been taken from me' or 'My good has been withheld from me'—then you will expand into that place which Isaac called "Rehoboth." It will be your place of enlargement, and of greater expression.

When you have expanded sufficiently in consciousness to a broad place, there will be no negative experiences to try to claim your good. After this third well named "Rehoboth" was dug, Isaac exclaimed, "For now Jehovah hath made room for us, and we shall be fruitful in the land." (Genesis 26:22) It is in such a broad place in consciousness that you demonstrate vast benefits as never before!

Isaac was so grateful that they were able to keep this well that he built an altar to Jehovah and rendered thank offerings. Jehovah promised to bless Isaac in return. (Genesis 26:24, 25)

After Isaac's herdsmen discovered this well, the Philistines appeared for a different reason: They wanted to make peace with Isaac. As they approached, Isaac asked them, "Why have you come, since you hate me and sent me away from you?" (Genesis 26:27) They replied, "We see plainly that Jehovah is with thee . . . Let us make a covenant with thee, that thou will do us no hurt, as we have not touched thee, and as we have done unto thee nothing but good, and have sent thee away in peace; thou art now the blessed of Jehovah." (Genesis 26:28, 29)

Isaac might have argued the point with them when they claimed they had not hurt him; that they had done nothing but good to him, even though they had taken his wells from him, and had pushed him out of their land. They had also demanded reconciliation with him. But Isaac seemed pleased that these troublesome Philistines wanted peace at last. He prepared a feast for them and asked them to remain overnight as his guests. The next morning they departed in peace.

In the East overnight hospitality is given only to those people who are regarded as lifetime friends. Isaac's generosity indicated complete reconciliation with the Philistines.

Isaac's Fourth Well of Abundance

From Isaac's experiences we observe why you can afford to be nonresistant, even to the most demanding "Philistines" that may appear in your life. When you are, your good overflows. As soon as the Philistines departed in peace, Isaac's servants rushed in to say they had just dug another well and had found water! Isaac victoriously named this place "'Beer-sheba" which meant "well of fulfillment."

After you have been tested and have reacted with nonresistance, then comes fulfillment. If you have been seeking fulfillment and it has not come, do not give up hope. It is because you are still on your way into that bigger place in consciousness. When you are nonresistant and divinely indifferent to the Philistines—when you do not make a fuss about what they seem to take from you for a time—they have no permanent power over you. They finally depart in peace and you demonstrate your "well of fulfillment."

The Prospering Power of Agreement

You may have regarded nonresistance as an indifferent yielding to whatever occurred. You may have considered it a teaching fit only for the unfit, or as a practice suited only to those who are incapable of self defense. Most people have.

However, *nonresistance is stronger than resistance.* Its practice requires far more mind power than is required by fighting back. You resist what you oppose, criticize, or resent. *Resistance centers on detail.* Nonresistance accepts the generalization. When you resist a difficulty, you antagonize it and it fights back.

You probably know people who are constantly upset over details. They "cannot see the forest for the trees." Such people either die young or suffer from ill health, emotional stress, or financial problems caused by their own fretful attitudes.

How can you refrain from criticism and resentment to a situation that is not being handled right? If you will agree where you can agree and refrain from dwelling upon points that you cannot accept, you will keep in harmony with your inner self and with the universe. *Always there is ground for agreement. Agree or withdraw in peace.*

This is the prosperity lesson you learn from the peaceful millionaire, Isaac. He did not become upset by apparent injustices. He did not fight for his rights. He withdrew in peace and dug deeper wells in consciousness. Isaac went deeper within his own being each time to meet the challenges presented him by the hostile Philistines. As he looked for grounds for agreement and refused to fight back, it is little wonder that his income increased a hundredfold in just one year! *Isaac knew that no one could take his good from him, and that that which was his by Divine Right would come to him under "divine timing."*

How Businesswoman Prospered Through Using The Power of Agreement

A businesswoman found herself exposed in business to a man who always talked about poverty and financial limitation. This made her feel poor and her business was affected.

In order to demonstrate increased supply, she knew she must feel prosperous because *a feeling of opulence precedes opulent results.*

She had disliked the businessman who made her feel poor. She had blamed her dwindling business on him. Then she reversed her thinking. She began to bless this man. Every time she thought of him she would say to herself, "THIS MAN IS IN MY LIFE FOR MY GOOD AND FOR MY PROSPERITY."

Through this same man, she soon met a client for whom she performed a business service. In return the client paid her several thousand dollars. The troublesome man soon moved to a distant city, and faded out of her life harmoniously.

This businesswoman proved that when you agree with the good in a situation—whether you can see the good there or not—and when you consider likenesses instead of differences, then your life becomes frictionless and your growth is unaccompanied by pain.

How Businessman Prospered Through Agreement

A businessman often said, "I BAPTIZE EVERY EVENT IN MY LIFE WITH THE SAME NAME. IF I HAVE A FAILURE, I CALL IT A SUCCESS, AND EVENTUALLY IT PROVES TO BE A SUCCESS."

Isaac proved this. As he kept moving on nonresistantly, he expanded into his own true place of fulfillment. But each experience that had seemed one of failure had actually been an experience in success, because it had pushed him on to a bigger place that became one of fulfillment.

Go back in your thinking to those experiences in which you thought you failed. Rename them a success. They *were* because they prodded you on to greater good.

Jesus said, "Agree with thine adversary quickly." (Matthew 5:25) When you agree with an adverse situation of the past or present, and are undisturbed by it, it has no power to hurt you and it fades out.

Baptize that situation as "good." Pronounce it good regardless of what it appears to be. Find some point of agreement with it. You will be victorious in meeting it, and you will be prospered by it, as you do this.

How The Power of Agreement Worked On A Complaining Wife

At the end of her first year of marriage, a young wife decided the time had come to tell her husband about all of his faults. "Now that we've been married a year, we should be able to be honest with each other," she said to her husband. "I am going to point out all your faults to you, dear. Then you can point out all my faults to me."

She recited a long list of woes about her husband, all of which centered on details. Then she said, "Now it's your turn. Tell me what is wrong with me."

This nonresistant husband wisely replied, "You are perfect in every way, and I would not have one thing about you changed."

Silence fell upon this woman's lips. She inwardly vowed that never again would she allow herself to think that her husband had any faults.

When you find yourself in the midst of negative experiences ask, "What details am I resisting, opposing, or criticizing?"

Dwell on likenesses, not differences. Look for something to agree with in the situation. Agree with it and withdraw in peace. By doing so, you keep your peace of mind. You become victor instead of victim to the experiences through which you have passed.

How Cruelty In Marriage Was Healed

A wife had what she considered to be a very cruel husband. She kept trying to find something good about him but his cruelty overpowered everything else. She began to realize that by thinking of him as cruel, she was giving his cruelty emotional power.

She decided she must find something about him with which she could agree. She decided that if she refused to allow his cruelty to upset her, and if she refused to feed it mental or emotional power, his cruelty would fade away for lack of attention. She realized that *the only way a negative condition can remain in force is for someone to continue to feel badly about it.*

Then she remembered how kind he was to their dog! She reasoned that anyone who was that kind to animals could not be all bad. This was the point of agreement she held to when old criticisms of him tried to flare up.

As she deliberately dwelled upon this one good trait, other of his commendable qualities came to her attention. As her attitude toward her husband began to improve, he subconsciously responded. His previous cruelty toward her gradually lessened, so that harmony and peace finally existed between them again.

The success law of agreement says: Be undisturbed by a situation and it will dissolve from neglect. When you can no longer be disturbed, all inharmony will disappear from your external world.

Isaac refused to be disturbed by the Philistines and they pushed him into a large place—a place of fulfillment. After they appeared one last time to make their peace with him, they faded away completely. Though this man of peace let them think they were having their own way, *he* was the ultimate victor!

Agreeing With A Former Marriage Brings A Happy One

One man had suffered through several unhappy marriages. A friend, who knew the success power of agreement, advised him to go back in his thinking to his first marriage, and to find some point of agreement with that marriage; then forgive that partner, and release the experience—baptizing that marriage a success.

When the man did this, he realized how much he still resented his first wife. That resentment had unconsciously been carried over and directed toward other matters, so that none of his marriages had worked out.

His mental treatment was, "I FORGIVE YOU. I RE-
LEASE YOU. OUR MARRIAGE WAS FOR GOOD.
OUR MARRIAGE WAS A SUCCESS BECAUSE WE
BOTH LEARNED FROM IT." For each succeeding marriage, he gave the same mental treatment until he felt a
sense of peace. When he later married again, it proved to
be one of fulfillment. He named it a success from the start
as he often looked for points of agreement.

Do not say that you have "failed in marriage," or that
you have "failed in business," or that you are in "failing
health." *You have never failed in any experience because
you learned something from it.* So long as you keep your
thoughts upon personal troubles of the past or present, you
bind them to you. When you name them a success and look
upward, the forces of heaven rush to your aid.

*How A Bereaved Woman Got A Job Through
The Prospering Power of Agreement*

A woman was curt and rude to a widow. The bereaved
woman used nonresistance on the thoughtless acquaintance:
"I will remember only how kind you have been to me in
the past. There are many nice things to remember about
you, so it does not matter what you say to me now."

The previously rude woman soon surprised the widow by
finding a job for her just when she needed it most.

When you are nonresistant to negative appearances and
given them no power, this opens the way for your good
to still appear.

A Mental Treatment For Invoking The Prospering Power of Agreement

When you are in a millionaire consciousness of supply, you need not fight for your good, nor compete for it. Like Isaac, you will find yourself unfolding into your place of fulfillment.

For this purpose declare often: "ALWAYS THERE IS GROUND FOR AGREEMENT. I FIND SOME POINT OF AGREEMENT AND DWELL UPON IT. I THINK ABOUT LIKENESSES, NOT DIFFERENCES. I BAPTIZE EVERY SITUATION IN MY LIFE A SUCCESS. I HAVE NEVER FAILED BECAUSE I HAVE LEARNED FROM EACH EXPERIENCE. EVERY EXPERIENCE IN MY LIFE HAS BEEN A SUCCESSFUL ONE. WHEN I AM UNDISTURBED BY APPEARANCES, THAT WHICH IS WORTHWHILE REMAINS. THAT WHICH IS NO LONGER OF VALUE FADES AWAY. WHEN I AM NONRESISTANT TOWARD MY GOOD, IT COMES TO MEET ME FROM EVERY DIRECTION AND THROUGH EVERY EXPERIENCE. KNOWING THIS, I REJOICE AS I NOW EXPERIENCE THE P R O S P E R I N G POWER OF AGREEMENT."

SUMMARY

1. Isaac became so wealthy that the Philistines envied him. When you begin to prosper and others envy you, follow Isaac's example and do not fight back. You can become victor over such envy if you declare often, "LOVE ENVIETH NOT. THE PROSPERING TRUTH HAS SET ME FREE TO PROSPER ABUNDANTLY."

2. Isaac's secret for increasing his income a hundredfold in one year lies in the fact that he was nonresistant to his foes. He refused to waste time and energy fighting back.

3. His nonresistance formed a vacuum, which quickly acted as a magnet to attract greater good to him.

4. Isaac knew that becoming inwardly still in the face of disturbing situations was the surest way to deliverance from them.

5. The Philistines were envious of Isaac's wealth and asked him to leave. With his unlimited resources he could have retaliated. Instead he released this valuable land and moved on.

6. After he departed into the Valley of Gerar, his herdsmen dug wells there and elsewhere. The Valley of Gerar meant "a halting place." Isaac knew this symbolized a halting place in his growth, not a place in which he wished to settle.

7. The metaphysical meaning of the names of those wells gives us the clue to his successful use of the law of agreement.

8. The first well was named "Esek" which meant "coming in touch with substance." Isaac knew that in the expansion of his prosperity consciousness, he was beginning to come in touch with the inner flow of substance, but he did not have to settle for this limited amount. By releasing this well, he expanded into a great place of supply.

9. The second well was named "Sitnah" which meant "strife, contention, oppression." To try to hang on to this well would have only caused strife and contention. He released it to the Philistines, too, and moved on.

10. He named the third well "Rehoboth" which meant "a broad place, enlargement, greater expression, expansion of thought." The Philistines did not try to take this well. Instead they wanted to make peace with Isaac. When you expand into your true place, negative experiences fade away.

11. Isaac named the fourth well "Beersheba" which meant "well of fulfillment." In that bigger place in consciousness, you find fulfillment and peace.

12. From Isaac we learn: Always there is ground for agreement. Agree or withdraw in peace. There is healing, prospering, harmonizing power in this success law of agreement.

THE PERSISTENT MILLIONAIRE-- JACOB

HIS PROSPERITY SECRETS FOR YOU

— Chapter 5 —

"Jacob started out poor, but he ended up rich," wrote one historian. We might add, "Very rich." He became a millionaire through persistence.

Jacob has often been depicted as the naughty boy of the Old Testament. All of his bad points have been pointed out, and few of his good ones. When viewed impartially, his life is a tremendous study in the use of the universal prosperity principles that were known and practiced in ancient times, and that are still available to you today.

Although Jacob has usually been described as cold-blooded, crafty, and deceitful, he was patient in disappointment. He turned to God for guidance in his extreme experiences. Jehovah never reprimanded Jacob for his shrewdness. Jacob gradually learned how to use his mind powers rightly so that he went on to outstanding success. Jehovah finally renamed Jacob "Israel" which meant "Prince of God."

Most of us can identify with Jacob, who started out using his mind powers from a human standpoint to try to force his good. When you first learn of the tremendous results you can obtain through the deliberate use of mind power, you may often try to use it to force your good too. Later Jacob learned to use his mind powers constructively and so can you—as you grow into it. He had many a bitter struggle but he prevailed and won out.

Jacob's Problems Began Because of Prosperity

Jacob's problems began when he stole his brother's birthright, which included a prosperity blessing that Jacob wanted:

> "God give thee of the dew of heaven and the fatness of the earth, and plenty of corn and wine. Let people serve thee, and nations bow down to thee."
>
> (Genesis 27:28, 29)

We are all interested in receiving this prosperity blessing, because the "dew of heaven" symbolizes rich ideas. The "fatness of the earth" symbolizes rich results. You may receive this prosperity blessing, which is your birthright, by affirming often: "I AM NOW BLESSED WITH 'THE DEW OF HEAVEN' AS RICH IDEAS. I AM NOW BLESSED WITH 'THE FATNESS OF THE EARTH' AS RICH RESULTS."

Prospering Power of Release Comes First

Jacob was still in a human consciousness of prosperity where he thought he had to fight for his good, to cheat, and to scheme for it. His actions caused so many problems with his family that he "left the scene of the crime."

His father forgave him before he left home. Isaac even bestowed a prosperity blessing upon his erring son, one fit for a millionaire—which Jacob persisted in becoming:

"God Almighty bless thee, and make thee fruitful . . . And give thee the blessing of Abraham . . . that thou mayest inherit the land of thy sojournings, which God gave unto Abraham." (Genesis 28:3, 4)

The first prosperity principles that Jacob used were those of release of mistakes and forgiveness. He released his mistakes by leaving home and going elsewhere to try again, after his father generously forgave him, and even bestowed a prosperity blessing upon him.

Like Jacob, when you have erred, instead of hanging onto those mistakes, release them, and make a fresh start. You can do so by declaring, "THE FORGIVING LOVE OF THE UNIVERSE HAS SET ME FREE FROM ALL MISTAKES OF THE PAST OR PRESENT. I FACE THE FUTURE WISE, FREE, AND UNAFRAID."

When Isaac forgave his son for having deceived him, he also bestowed a prosperity blessing upon Jacob that described his inheritance. You can claim your inheritance of universal abundance by declaring often, "I AM NOW COME INTO MY RICH INHERITANCE OF HEALTH, WEALTH, AND HAPPINESS. I AM. I AM. I AM."

When Jacob left his familiar surroundings, he left behind him the usual human methods for trying to demonstrate prosperity. He stopped scheming, cheating, and trying to force his good. He went forth endowed with the prosperity blessing given by his father, who had graciously forgiven and released him.

How Release Brought Gift of A Grand Piano

Like Jacob, you may have expected your good to come to you in one set of circumstances, only to find it elsewhere, after you have released the former circumstances which have become non-productive.

A youthful musician had friends speak the word with him for a piano, which he needed in connection with his work. When the money did not appear for him to personally purchase such an instrument, he continued to affirm that it would come anyway. Though affirmations were often spoken over a period of months by some of his friends for "Jim's piano," nothing happened until he gave up a part-time job which had become increasingly dissatisfying.

Two weeks after he gained his release from that job, he spent the weekend with relatives in a distant city. Together they attended several special musical events. Afterwards, as he was preparing to board a plane to return home, one of his relatives said, "You love music so much that I have decided to make you a gift of the best piano you can find. Let me know when you have located it and I will send you a check."

He shopped extensively until he found just the right instrument. When a music professor later saw this piano, he assured the young musician it *was* the best piano in town! But this rich gift only came after he had gained release from a nonproductive situation.

The Prospering Power of Getting Definite

After he released his former surroundings and former mistakes, Jacob started out to Haran to work for his uncle. Enroute he used another success principle when he made a Success Covenant with God. (Chapter 6 describes this method in detail.) This act indicated that he was not only sorry for his mistakes, but that he wanted God's help in his new venture.

In his Success Covenant, Jacob got definite about what he wanted to experience in his life. He proved that it pays to get definite, because God granted him far more than he had asked.

A widow lived on a small annuity plus a Social Security income. Then she decided it was foolish to be content with such a meager existence. She got definite in her words about what she wanted and began to declare every day: "LARGE SUMS OF MONEY AND BIG HAPPY FINANCIAL SURPRISES NOW COME TO ME FOR MY PERSONAL USE. I USE THEM WISELY."

Her daughter soon invited her for a visit. It would cost $100 to make the trip. Though there seemed no way for this extra amount to come, the widow accepted the invitation in faith, and spoke her prosperity decrees daily.

She soon heard from the Social Security Administration. They stated that her next check would include an increase that was due her. When the accumulated back-income arrived, it was a check for $113 given in addition to her usual check. She quickly bought a plane ticket and joined her daughter for a happy visit.

The Prospering Power of Dwelling Upon Substance

After making his Success Covenant, Jacob journeyed to Paddan-aram in the Land of Haran to work for his uncle. The word "Paddan-aram" symbolizes the unlimited substance of the universe, which is the source of all outer wealth. "Paddan-aram" also symbolizes the mind power that is necessary to manifest that substance as visible results.

Many people know that universal substance is the inner source of all outer wealth. Unlike Jacob, they do not persist mentally until it manifests as visible results in their financial affairs and elsewhere.

A housewife decided to test the power of substance in a trying situation. She related:

"My husband and I were coming home from a trip. I had a seven-months old baby, and our car quit running in the Pennsylvania mountains, miles from anything. It was getting dark, the baby was crying, and my husband was getting mad. When he looked under the hood, he could find no reason why the car had stopped.

"Quietly to myself I began to say, 'DIVINE SUBSTANCE IS THE ONE AND ONLY REALITY IN THIS SITUATION. DIVINE SUBSTANCE IS APPROPRIATELY MANIFESTING FOR US HERE AND NOW.'

"When my husband got back in the car and tried the ignition, the car started. All the way home he kept saying, 'I sure don't get it.' I kept quiet and silently thanked Divine Substance for its help."

The word "Haran" means "uplifted." Jacob got into an exalted state of mind by dwelling upon Divine Substance as the Source of his supply in the land of Haran. The ancient people knew the power of thinking about substance thereby drawing success to them. Like Jacob, when you find yourself in strange new circumstances—or in trying ones—that is the time to dwell upon Divine Substance as the one and only reality.

Karmic Debts Must Be Paid In Order To Prosper

After Jacob began working for his uncle in the land of Haran, the first thing that happened was a surprise. He reaped an unhappy result, yet it proved to be a part of a prospering process that was working for him.

When his uncle had asked, "What shall thy wages be?" (Genesis 29:15) the financial arrangement had been, "I will serve thee seven years for Rachel, thy daughter." (Genesis 29:18) And he did. Yet he was deceived by finding himself married to Leah, the eldest daughter. He found it necessary to work 7 more years for Rachel.

The law of cause and effect was at work from his previous actions: He had cheated in the past and now he was being cheated in return.

When you begin to develop an expanded conciousness of prosperity, often you have to clear up karmic debts which you have incurred from the past, before you are free to be personally prospered. Your early prosperity demonstrations may go to other people, or to outside situations that seem unfair—yet never are. You are paying off debts from the past, either from earlier in this life, or from some previous one.

Yet *when you meet disappointing experiences constructively, you always go forward to greater good.*

When you are cheated or your good is withheld from you,
it may be that like Jacob, you cheated or withheld someone else's good in the past. An old score is being settled.

Instead of whining, "This is a terrible injustice. I have
been cheated," say to yourself, "I have paid for past mistakes through this present disappointment, so I now meet
this disappointing experience constructively, and I go forward to greater good." Do not waste time and energy fighting the present disappointment. If you do, you bog down in
failure.

The law of cause and effect often bobs up to be paid off
and cleared away when you begin unfolding your prosperity
consciousness.

If you meet those karmic debts nonresistantly and pay
them off, you are then free to be permanently prospered.
But if you fight and resist them—they often appear again
and again in the form of unforeseen and unwanted re-
sponsibilities. This holds you down to a lower state of consciousness where you are never truly prospered.

Jacob paid his karmic debt by working 14 years for
Rachel.

How Picturing Made Them Rich

Jacob later asked for a financial settlement from his uncle
because he wanted to return home. His uncle did not want
to free him because Jacob was making Laban rich. Laban
asked Jacob to state his wage. Jacob asked for all the
speckled and spotted cattle that would be born in the flock,

so that he could start his own herd, and begin to feel financially independent.

Laban agreed that Jacob was to have all the future spotted cattle that were born for his own herd. It soon became apparent that Laban had no intention of sharing his flock with Jacob, though Jacob had made him rich. Instead, Laban secretly ordered the spotted female animals removed from the flock, leaving only the plain ones which he assumed would reproduce plain cattle.

To keep from being cheated out of his good, Jacob used the picturing power of the mind. (Abraham, you recall, had used this same prosperity principle when he had been cheated out of the fertile land by Lot.) Jacob took fresh poplar rods and peeled some white streaks in them. He placed these streaked rods around the watering troughs where the herd conceived, and they brought forth ring-streaked, speckled cattle.

Jacob proved that you can picture your good and have it quietly come to you regardless of what others about you are saying or doing.

Jacob increased his uncle's flock first, and then his own, through imaging. He reminded his uncle, "Thou had little before I came. It has increased into a multitude, and the Lord has blessed thee since my coming." (Genesis 30:30)

When your good is withheld from you, instead of fighting, arguing, or trying to reason with anyone to make it come to pass, just picture the desired results. As Jacob proved, you can image your good and bring it through rather than trying to reason it through or force it through. You can hasten your good through picturing it!

Imaging was a well-known success technique among the ancient people. The wealth Jacob acquired through the picturing power of the mind is described: "And the man grew exceedingly rich and had much cattle, maidservants, manservants, camels, asses." (Genesis 30:43)

How A Father Made Comeback After Daughter's Death

A businessman was heartbroken over the death of his daughter. He had been unable to pull himself together and his business dwindled, until he learned of the prospering power of pictures.

He made a success map picturing the financial success he needed to survive. At the top of his success map he placed these words, on which he meditated daily: "DIVINE SUBSTANCE CANNOT BE WITHHELD FROM ME NOW. DIVINE SUBSTANCE CANNOT BE TAKEN FROM ME NOW. I PICTURE MY WAY TO PROSPERITY, AND MY ABUNDANT GOOD QUICKLY MANIFESTS NOW." Soon afterwards, he began to rise out of his emotional slump and his business became more prosperous than ever. His new-found success proved therapeutic in overcoming his former grief.

How To Claim Your Freedom From Experiences You've Outgrown

Laban and his sons finally became so jealous of Jacob's wealth that Jacob decided to leave the country and return home, even though Laban did not want to release him. Jacob had to claim his freedom by just leaving anyway.

When you have learned all you can from an experience, after you have demonstrated prosperity in it and after you have helped others to achieve satisfactory results, you will probably grow out of that experience. If that experience does not want to release you, you will have to claim your freedom from it anyway. You can begin doing so by declaring, "MY SUCCESS CANNOT BE LIMITED, SO I AM NOW FREED TO THE NEXT STEP IN MY PROGRESS, GROWTH, AND SUCCESS."

Your success is progressive. When you have reached certain stages in your growth, others around you may become hostile to your success. Often you will find, like Jacob, that you have completed the phase of your growth due from that experience. You have outgrown that present experience and are ready to move on into new circumstances, where you will be able to expand rapidly without restraint or interference by others.

At such times it helps to declare, "MY SUCCESS IS PROGRESSIVE. I NOW GO FROM SUCCESS TO GREATER SUCCESS, QUICKLY AND IN PEACE."

The divine dissatisfaction arising at such times is good, because it gives you the incentive needed to dare to launch forth into new and untried experiences elsewhere.

First Comes Release, Then Vast Improvement

On the way home, Jacob sent his family and possessions ahead and he stayed behind at the Ford of Jabbok, where he wrestled with the angel until daybreak.

At every forward step in man's evolution, he gives up present ideas and possessions, so that he may receive greater ones. First, Jacob had released his uncle as a channel of his supply. Then he even dared to send his family and possessions on ahead. He released everything.

When major changes come, you may have to release everything connected with a past cycle: Income, possessions, people. This act of release frees you to receive your expanded good in new situations.

Jacob's wrestling with the angel symbolized his own doubts and fears; he was wrestling with his Higher Self as he released all he had attained. Such an inner struggle was natural. The person who desires to have his good expanded is often disciplined in this way. As he gains his emotional perspective, the discipline from it opens the way to his expanded good.

How Inner Success Must Be Balanced With Outer Results

When Jacob started homeward, he made his peace with his brother, Esau, by sending rich gifts of cattle ahead. Esau did not need these gifts because he had become wealthy in his own right. Although he had earlier threatened to kill Jacob if he ever returned, he graciously accepted the advance gifts from his brother and they were harmoniously reunited.

Jacob knew that willingness to make peace with a former enemy is a necessity for success. Whereas Jacob symbolizes mind power, his twin brother, Esau, symbolizes the physical side of life.

People often work hard mentally, as Jacob had, to achieve success, but there comes a time when their mind powers must be reunited with the physical side of life in order to balance them and their success. People who do not get this balance can suffer from mental, emotional, physical, and financial difficulties.

112 THE MILLIONAIRES OF GENESIS

True success is both mental and physical. Esau (physical) and Jacob (mental) needed each other for their mutual benefit and balance. Their harmonious reunion gave them that balance.

At Height of His Wealth, Jacob Gave Thanks

After reunion with Esau, Jacob settled down in his homeland. He secured a parcel of land where he pitched his tents. There he erected an altar because he knew the time had come to give thanks.

The act of erecting an altar indicates that he gave a "thank offering" or, perhaps, a tithe to God: 1) In appreciation for his vast wealth; 2) To give it a divine protection.

All that he had asked for years earlier in his Success Covenant had come to him: Guidance, protection, a satisfying way of life, a large household, vast wealth, reconciliation with his family, and return to his homeland. He wisely felt that the time had come to give thanks publicly.

How A Housewife and A Man In Retirement Prospered

With Jacob, many others have found there is a prospering protection in the act of giving. A retired businessman explained his continuing high income in this way:

"Although I retired in 1957, each year since then my income has increased. The past year was the best ever—more than double any I had even while on a payroll. I attribute my growing income to the consistent act of tithing. I have continued to tithe a tenth of my gross income since retirement just as before. My retirement income continues to grow."

A housewife said, "Tithing works! We find our bills being paid and there is some left over each month in spite of the rising costs of living."

Jacob's Later Years Were Spent Amid Vast Wealth

After his son, Joseph, became a billionaire as Prime Minister of Egypt, Jacob went there to live amid vast wealth. For many years he enjoyed tremendous prestige as father of the popular Joseph. At Jacob's passing, the Egyptians paid him special homage as. father of their beloved Prime Minister.

When you persist toward success through the constructive use of your mind power, like Jacob, your present success finally supplants and replaces all previous failures. Life forgives you for past mistakes. Life becomes rewarding and satisfying for you. You can persist into success by declaring often: "LIFE NOW FORGIVES ME FOR ALL PAST MISTAKES. LIFE NOW BECOMES REWARDING AND SATISFYING FOR ME. I AM GRATEFUL."

The Basic Success Secret You Learn From Jacob's Life

Jacob met life "head on" early in his unfoldment. He fought for his good, schemed for it, and mentally outwitted others for it. Life seemed to get the best of him for a time, but he got practice out of it.

A surface defeat may contain the germ of transcendent success. Certainly Jacob's surface defeats and disappointments became the foundation for his later successes in life. It can be so for you too!

Jacob, symbolizing mind power, had a quick, brilliant alert mind. As already pointed out, he knew the power of thought, the power of suggestion, the power of picturing what he wanted. He used all of these success principles to make Laban and himself wealthy.

But in the process, Jacob had many human relations problems to face, work out, overcome in spite of his tremendous mental abilities.

There was a good reason for this: Even though a person has a brilliant mind and great knowledge of the laws of mind action, that person is not balanced mentally, spiritually, emotionally, and physically until he balances that mind power with love. Mind must express through love in order to be productive of good. Mind power can become scheming, crafty, plotting, deceitful, even unreasonable, when it is not balanced with love.

Why Brilliant People May Have Human Relations Problems

Often a person learns about the power of thought and begins to develop it constructively. Then human relations problems appear. When this happens, mind power is being given an opportunity to be balanced through love. When it is, problems are resolved and balance comes.

If you know people who have developed the power of thought and yet are faced with human relations problems, this can be the reason. Your first reaction may be, "If they are so advanced in this way of thinking, why are they having human relations problems?"

It is because they *are* so advanced mentally that they have those problems. They are having to do their emotional homework, so that their mind power can be balanced by love.

In your own experience, do not turn your back on human relations problems when they appear. Do not try to by-pass them. Meet them nonresistantly with love, so that a balancing process may take place in your interior nature. This balancing process will always lead you into your expanded good.

Your growth and expansion comes in phases of normality. First you gain knowledge of the creative power of thought and begin to use it mentally. Then human relations problems often arise so that you may prove it in the heart, or emotionally. There is no balance in your consciousness until love and wisdom are united in you and reflected in your life. *If you have been mentally fighting something in your life, rest your overworked mind, and think in terms of love and peace instead.* As you practice doing this daily, the results can amaze you!

How To Realize Your Heart's Desires

When Jacob balanced his fantastic mind power with love, when he met all kinds of human relations problems through love, he was able to realize his heart's desires. Balance came into his personality and into his life.

Take anything in your life that seems not to be going well. Spend a few minutes each day thinking about that situation constructively. Bless it with the thought of love and peace. Remind yourself that harmony and true success are the divine purpose of your life.

Do not fight, manipulate, or dictate. Do not try mentally to force anything or anybody in the matter. Treat people and events involved with thoughts of love and peace.

As you follow this daily practice, instead of becoming eccentric, rigid, demanding, you will become more flexible, adaptable, loving, harmonious, and successful in every phase of your life.

From Jacob you learn to think on what you have—not on what you have lost. Blessings that are recognized and counted multiply! Every lost thing can be restored or compensated for in the course of your growth into success.

You may wish to meditate often upon these statements characterized in the life of Jacob. As you do so, may you realize your heart's desires:

"I NOW WILLINGLY COOPERATE WITH PEOPLE, SITUATIONS, AND WITH LIFE. AND PEOPLE, SITUATIONS, AND LIFE NOW COOPERATE WITH ME. I AM DIVINELY EQUIPPED TO MEET SUCCESS-FULLY EVERY EXPERIENCE THAT LIFE DE-MANDS OF ME. AS I MEET EACH SITUATION WITH LOVE AND PEACE, THEN WISDOM AND LOVE ARE UNITED IN ME. I REMEMBER THE MARVELOUS POWER OF KINDNESS. AS I ADD TO THE HAPPINESS OF OTHERS THROUGH KIND-NESS, THAT KINDNESS OVERCOMES ALL FRIC-TION IN MY LIFE. I SHUN THE ECCENTRIC. I MEET DISAPPOINTING EXPERIENCES CON-STRUCTIVELY, AND I ALWAYS GO FORWARD TO GREATER GOOD!"

SUMMARY

1. Most of us can identify with Jacob, who symbolizes mind power. When we first learn of the power of thought, like Jacob, we are inclined to use it to try to force our good. However, Jacob went on to outstanding success when he learned to use his mind power constructively, and so can we.

2. After Jacob stole his brother's prosperity blessing, he released his mistake by leaving home. His father generously forgave him and bestowed a blessing upon hm before he left.

3. Enroute to work for his uncle, Jacob got definite by making a Success Covenant with God. This indicated that he was sorry for his mistakes and wanted God's help in the future.

4. In "Paddan-aram," in the land of Haran, Jacob got into an uplifted state of mind by dwelling upon Divine Substance as the Source of his supply. Like Jacob, the ancient people all knew that, by dwelling upon substance, they could draw success to them.

5. The first thing that happened to Jacob in Haran was a surprise. The law of cause and effect worked from his past actions. He was deceived into marrying Leah when he thought he had married Rachel. Jacob paid his karmic debt by working fourteen years for Rachel.

6. When his uncle tried to cheat him financially, Jacob used the picturing power of the mind to produce the spotted cattle that had been promised him. He proved that you can picture your good and have it come to you regardless of what others about you are saying or doing.

7. Jacob made himself and his uncle wealthy through the picturing power of the mind.

8. Jacob finally realized he had outgrown his relationship with his uncle and he wanted to be financially free from him. When his uncle did not want to release him, he left anyway because he knew his success was progressive and he must expand.

9. After releasing his uncle as his former channel of income, he also released his family and vast possessions, sending them on ahead while he remained behind. His Higher Self (angel) wrestled with his own doubts over this vast change and won out.

10. After being harmoniously reunited with his brother Esau, indicating that success is both mental (Jacob) and physical (Esau), Jacob did not forget to give thanks. All that he had asked for years earlier had been given him.

11. His later years were spent amid vast wealth in Egypt where he enjoyed tremendous prestige as father of the popular Prime Minister, Joseph.

12. When you persist toward success, through the constructive use of your mind powers, like Jacob, your present success finally supplants and replaces all previous failures. Life becomes rewarding and satisfying.

THE PROSPERING POWER
OF A
SUCCESS COVENANT

HOW TO MAKE ONE

— Chapter 6 —

The German philosopher, Goethe, once advised, "What you can do or dream you can, begin it. Boldness has genius, power, and magic in it." The way to help your dreams come true is by making a Success Covenant.

Jacob made one at a crucial time in his life. Abraham, Hannah, and other Biblical figures made covenants with God that were equally successful during trying periods in their lives.

At the time Jacob made his success covenant with God, he had every strike against him. He had cheated his brother, hurt his mother, and disappointed his father. His brother had even threatened to kill him.

119

After disgracing himself in the eyes of his family, Jacob left their rich household. At this point, Jacob had nothing—not even a good reputation. He was past 40 years of age. Enroute to Haran, this outcast son sank down exhausted in body, depressed in spirit, and slept. He interpreted his famous dream with the angels ascending and descending the ladder as an omen of forgiveness and of success that could still be his.

Upon awakening, Jacob wasted no time in making his famous Success Covenant with God. Jacob intuitively knew that man can be what he determines to be; that he can be master or he can be serf. Jacob seemed to know, even at that low point in his life, that it rests with man whether he shall fill the high places in life or the low ones—whether he shall serve or be served—lead or be led, be sickly or healthy, poor or wealthy.

There lies within most people a divine desire to excel, to succeed. This divine desire for success should be encouraged and developed constructively. Jacob did this by first making his Success Covenant.

JACOB'S SUCCESS COVENANT

Jacob's Success Covenant was in 2 parts:

In *Part I,* Jacob specified what he wished God to help him accomplish: Prosperity, guidance, peace of mind, reconciliation with his family.

"Jacob vowed a vow: If God will be with me, and keep me in the way that I go, and will give me bread to eat, and raiment to put on, so that I come again to my father's house in peace, and Jehovah will be my God . . ."

In *Part II,* Jacob specified what he would do for God:
"Of all that thou shalt give me, I will surely give the
tenth unto thee."

(Genesis 28:20-22)

Often we have been inclined to tell God what we wanted
Him to do for us in life, then we selfishly stopped there. We
did not go all the way and agree with God what we would
do for Him in return, and in appreciation.

A "covenant" is a solemn agreement, usually between 2
people, to do specific things and to achieve specific results.
But such a covenant doesn't mean much unless *both* parties
do their part.

Jacob's covenant worked. God granted him far more than
he sought. When he returned to his father's house years
later he returned in peace, a very wealthy man.

Yet at the time Jacob made his Success Covenant in that
desolate place, to all appearances he was asking for the im-
possible: Prosperity, protection, guidance, and reconciliation with his family. Under the circumstances, his requests
seemed preposterous. He was out of favor with God and
man.

But Jacob took no chances. After making his large requests in *Part I* of his covenant, Jacob then did what most
people overlook. In *Part II* he stated specifically what he
would do for God, and he got busy fulfilling his part of
the covenant. He did not wait around to see what God was
going to do for him. He took it for granted that as he fulfilled his part of the agreement, God could be trusted to
produce the blessings sought. His method worked. Over the
years, God granted him far more than he sought in his
covenant!

Why A Success Covenant Works

Many success books talk about the power of writing down your desired good and then praying for guidance about its manifestation. People have often had marvelous results from use of this success technique.

But if that technique has not done for you what you think it should have, it is time you took that technique a step further. It is time to get specific and ask a loving Father for the blessings in life you desire. This you should do, because it is your heritage.

But do not stop there. Do your part by following through on the second step: Covenant with God what you plan to get busy doing for Him right away. After Jacob specified what he wished God to do for him, he balanced his requests by stating what he would do for God in return. When he got busy fulfilling his part of the covenant, it worked.

Often we have been inclined to tell God what we would do for Him later, *after* He has met our demands. Then we may have wondered why our good did not appear quickly. God cannot meet our demands fully under those terms, because we have not fulfilled our part of the covenant. We have not released any faith by getting busy doing something for God.

A Success Covenant is two-fold. Any lesser agreement is spiritually illegal because it is one-sided and unbalanced. People sometimes object, "I am not sure I like the idea of making a covenant with God for what I want. Isn't that 'bargaining' with God?"

No, because in a bargain you are trying to get something for nothing or almost nothing. In a covenant you are giving full measure for measure received. Any lesser agreement is a bargain; that's why it doesn't work. (Something for nothing is still nothing.)

How To Make A Success Covenant

When making a Success Covenant, it is wise to write it out. In Jacob's covenant, he "vowed a vow." This was important. In the Holy Land, even today, people place great importance upon "vowing a vow."

When a person undertakes a difficult task or is about to go on a hazardous journey, he first vows a vow. He asks God for protection, guidance, and supply. Then he vows what he will do for God in return for these blessings, and he gets busy fulfilling his part of the vow.

At the end of his journey, or at the end of the difficult task, the person who vowed a vow gives a thank offering or a tithe in appreciation for answered prayer. (As pointed out in Chapter 5, Jacob did this after returning to his homeland to live.)

To "vow a vow" is a sacred act which no person in the East would think of breaking. It is a serious, solemn agreement. During Biblical times, to break a vow that had been made voluntarily was even punishable by death.

The best way to "vow a vow" in your Success Covenant is to write it out. Even in ancient times, people placed great power upon the written word. They felt that by putting in writing how they wanted their lives to be, they reached past all fear and uncertainty into a higher realm of accomplishment.

Through your definite written words, you dissolve all obstacles and barriers on the visible and invisible planes of life. Your written words go out into the ethers of the universe to work through people, circumstances and events, to open the way for your desired good to come to pass.

When writing out your desires or "vowing a vow" in your Success Covenant, remember that the word "choice" is a magic word to the mind. Your mind constantly works through what you choose. Psychologists state that all things are done by choice. *Choice produces results, but it is up to you to choose what you want.*

How The Written Word Helps Doctor To Succeed

A doctor of chiropractic told me that for 20 years this had been his secret formula for success. At the time this doctor went into practice 2 decades ago, right out of college, he had nothing. But he and his wife believed that, if they consistently wrote down what they wanted in life, they would get it.

At the beginning of each New Year, instead of making New Year's resolutions of what they hoped the year might bring, they made a list of what they definitely *expected* the year to bring.

The first year they listed nice rental offices and a thriving practice. The second year they listed the purchase of business property on which they planned to build offices. Later they listed the purchase of a home and the birth of their first child. Another year their list included the acquisition of stocks, bonds, and other investments. Still later they listed a larger professional practice. Then their list included the purchase of a private plane, more cars, a boat.

From the first New Year's list this couple made, this method began to work for them! Once they had written down their desires for that particular year, they placed the list in their Bible, and simply gave thanks for the perfect results throughout the year. Several times by midyear the major items on their lists had come about. At other times, it was as late as December before the list began producing results. The year they listed the desire for their first child, she was born in October. Invariably their list-making method worked!

Today this couple has all the blessings they have put on their New Year's lists over the years: A fine practice and their own business property on which they have built beautiful offices. They now enjoy a lovely home, several cars, their own plane, additional financial assets such as stocks and bonds, and several healthy children who appeared first on their lists. The result is a healthy, happy, prosperous, spiritually-oriented family. As an elder in his church, this man has long been a tither.

Why You Should Get Specific

The importance of getting specific about what you want in your Success Covenant is shown in a study of the psychology of the poor. Psychological studies of poverty show that the poor are so caught up in their present problems that they do not plan ahead or think ahead. They spend most of their time and energies battling present circumstances. Also the poor often have great hostility and envy toward those people who succeed. The poor are inclined to resent success rather than to work in constructive ways to achieve it.

Another reason why you should get specific about what you want is because the soul of man must turn its attention outward, as well as inward, for balance. The soul is the blending area of the mind. Individuals who do not get definite in their thinking about what they want unconsciously continue to demonstrate what they do not want through absorbing the negative vibrations around them. They become confused, upset, and suffer from many needless problems, which have been subconsciously absorbed.

The great people of the Bible knew the power of getting definite. Jesus often specified healing, prosperity, and guidance for his followers.

Why By-Passing Part II Brings Failure

Too many people try to put off Part II of the covenant until *after* Part I has come to pass. To try to get something for nothing, or bargain with God in this way, usually leads to failure *and it should!*

A woman said, "I have some valuable property which I am trying to sell for one million dollars. Pray with me concerning the sale of this property and *when* it is sold, I will give a tithe of it to your ministry."

A tithe would have been $100,000.00. Yet this woman was not willing to give even $5 or $10 to God's work at the time she made that statement. So, of course, there was no way for her to expand her consciousness to receive one million dollars later and give $100,000.00 of it to His work. She never sold the property, but died leaving it for heirs to fight over. (Conversely, please note later in this Chapter how another woman made a Success Covenant and sold a piece of property for one million dollars.)

A man in the oil business said, "*When* I strike oil, I am going to give a tithe of the income from my oil wells to your church." Again this man was not giving $5 or $10 to God's work now, yet he thought he would be able to release thousands, maybe millions, to God's work later. He never struck oil. Instead he spent his life savings on oil leases and drilling equipment, only to strike "dry holes" or sand.

You may have been inclined to be like these people and to tell God what you would do for Him later, *after* He had met your demands. God cannot fully meet your demands under such terms, because you have not fulfilled your part of the covenant. Faith moves on substance, and you must do something as an act of faith in order for it to move on the substance of the universe and manifest increased abundance for you.

A businessman said, "I've made a fortune but I lost it. Now I owe Internal Revenue a million dollars. I cannot understand why God has not helped me. I prayed about this and I even gave my church $500.00."

Where you give is where you place your faith. If you do not give much, it indicates you do not have much faith in that area. You reap results accordingly. This man could still resolve his million dollar indebtedness, make another fortune and keep it, if he would enter into a Success Covenant and begin to do his part. By consistently tithing of his income, both now and later, he could be permanently prospered.

How Success Covenant Works For A Musician

A musician said, "After making a Success Covenant and beginning to tithe a tenth of my gross income to my church, I received an appointment to the piano faculty of one of the most famous schools of music in America. It is all the more remarkable that the position opened up just at the beginning of the school term, long after most vacancies are filled. It is even more unusual that I should have obtained it since I happen to be a member of the so-called 'minority race' for which such appointments are rare."

In addition to this job, this musician has a music studio where he does private tutoring. His public concerts are also thriving in this country and abroad.

Tourist Business Prospers Through Success Covenant

A man in the tourist business said, "I entered into a covenant with God at a time of business problems. Our business was family-owned and my father's drinking was wrecking our financial affairs. Our business was $30,000 in debt, and we were 3 mortgage payments behind on our beautiful home.

"It was at this hopeless point that I secretly made a Success Covenant with God, agreeing that I would give 10 per cent of all gross earnings from our business to His work. After I wrote our first tithe check, new customers began to stream in. Their visits brought new business and immediate cash. Several additional checks that were received through the mail made it possible to meet those back mortgage payments on our home. The way now seems to be opening for us to lease a motel which has unlimited financial potential, since it is located in a popular tourist area. The financial picture has quickly improved since I made that Success Covenant."

How A Lawyer's Success Covenant Prospered Him

A lawyer has made a Success Covenant at the beginning of each year since he first learned of this method in 1966. In that first Success Covenant, he wrote out in *Part I*: 1) That he wished help with the sale of a piece of property that had not sold for 2 years; 2) That he wished help with the sale of another piece of property that had not sold for 7 years; 3) That he wished guidance about some stocks whose value had been low; 4) That he wished help with certain court cases that had been pending for a long time.

In *Part II* of his covenant, this lawyer wrote out that he would begin immediately to tithe 10 per cent of all channels of his income. This would include the financial income from his law practice, the sale of property, the sale of stocks, income through inheritance, and any other income.

The first piece of property listed in *Part I* sold in a matter of weeks—after he had tried to sell it for 2 years. The second piece of property, which he had tried to sell for 7 years, sold in a matter of a few months, and at the highest price he had asked. The stocks, which had been low, rose in value and he sold them at more profit than he had dreamed of getting. The court cases listed in his covenant were harmoniously concluded.

This man has made his Success Covenant at the beginning of each New Year since with amazing results. Some years his covenant has worked even by midyear to produce the results stipulated.

He recently said, "I have proved that a Success Covenant works. This is a political year and a lot of people have a platform and a candidate. I do too. My candidate is Jacob, and my platform is his Success Covenant. I am actively campaigning for Jacob and his Success Covenant, because it's the greatest way in the world to become permanently prospered!"

You Can Test A Success Covenant In Small Ways First

If this Success Covenant idea seems too new to you to test it over a long period of time—like for a year—why not test it on a short term basis?

When one couple first heard of this method, they decided to make a covenant with God about just one item that concerned them. They later reported these results:

"We made a Success Covenant to sell our boat. It was a nice boat that we had gotten for our girls to use for water-skiing when they were growing up. Now they were both getting married about the same time, and we decided to sell it to help with wedding expenses. So we listed the sale of the boat in our Success Covenant.

"We were already tithing from our general income, but wrote out in our covenant that we would tithe from the sale of the boat too. My husband cleaned up the boat, thinking he would put an ad for its sale in the paper. He called a friend about this, but the friend knew of a man who wanted to buy the boat. The prospective buyer soon arrived, tried out the boat, and bought it! My husband asked $100 more than he expected to get. The purchaser talked him down $50.00. Even so, there was no expense for ads in the paper.

Nor was there the inconvenience of people streaming in and out to look at it. It had quickly sold to the first party that had been interested for $50 more than we had expected to receive."

Other Ways Of Invoking Part II of the Covenant

There are other ways you can invoke Part II of your covenant and do something for God besides tithe of your income. However, if you want to make a financial demonstration, you should open the way by proving your faith financially through tithing. Jacob did, and became a millionaire.

Working for your favorite charity, giving your time in volunteer work, or doing church work are some of the public service ways of invoking *Part II* of your covenant. Having regular periods of prayer, meditation, and inspirational study at home would be private ways of invoking *Part II* of your covenant.

A lady said, "I don't see why I should tithe my money to God's work. I tithe my time. I am a Sunday School teacher."

She was asked, "What are you trying to demonstrate? More time or more money?"

"I would like to have more time, but what I need most is more money." She got the point.

How To Assure Your Prosperity

If you would have your material affairs prosper, like Jacob you should agree with God to give one-tenth of your income to His work, and begin to do so promptly. If you keep your part of the agreement, you may rest assured that a loving Father will keep His and abundantly bless you. Many people have written out such contracts and put them away in the full assurance that the terms would be carried out by both parties. It has been found by everyone who has consistently used this method that it has been fulfilled.

A businesswoman needed work and made her covenant. She soon had 4 jobs, which she juggled successfully for a time. She finally gave up 3 of them and kept the fourth one. Her income has continued to expand. But none of these jobs came her way until she made her Success Covenant.

A businesswoman had inherited a piece of property that she had tried in vain to sell for one million dollars. Nothing happened until she learned about the prospering power of Success Covenants, and decided to make one. Soon after making that Success Covenant, she sold that piece of property for the long desired one million dollars! As agreed in her Success Covenant, she then shared one tenth of the sales price with the church where she had heard about Success Covenants. That church gratefully used her tithe of $100,000 in their building program. That businesswoman has continued to tithe and to prosper through use of the Success Covenants.

Like Jacob, when you bring God into your daily affairs you come into a Land where peace and plenty go hand in hand. For this purpose declare often: "AS I BRING GOD INTO MY DAILY AFFAIRS, I COME INTO A LAND WHERE PEACE AND PLENTY GO HAND IN HAND."

SPECIAL NOTE

For a free copy of the author's personalized Success Covenant, please write her.

SUMMARY

1. Jacob made a Success Covenant with God at a crucial time in his life and it worked. All that he asked for in it came to him.

2. Jacob's Success Covenant worked because it was balanced. In *Part I* he got specific in asking God for what he wanted and needed to succeed in life. In *Part II* he agreed what he would do for God, which was to tithe.

3. In like manner, the way to make your dreams come true is by making a Success Covenant.

4. When making a Success Covenant, it is wise to write it out. Through your definite written words, you dissolve all obstacles on the visible and invisible planes of life. Your written words go out into the ethers to work through people, circumstances and events, to open the way for your desired good to come to pass.

5. Choice produces results, but it's up to you to choose what you want.

6. In your Success Covenant, get definite about what you want and what you will do. Individuals who do not get definite about what they want unconsciously continue to demonstrate what they do not want through absorbing the negative vibrations around them.

7. You can test this Success Covenant method on a short term basis, to prove its power.

8. Along with tithing there are other ways of invoking Part II of the covenant: By agreeing to periods of daily prayer, meditation, inspirational study or perhaps to doing volunteer church work.

9. However, if you would have God prosper you in your material affairs, you should be proving your faith in His ability to help financially through the act of tithing.

10. Jacob made a Success Covenant at a time when he had every strike against him. Yet he succeeded. With God's help, through use of a Success Covenant, you can persist into your expanded good too.

THE FIRST BILLIONAIRE--
JOSEPH

HIS PROSPERITY SECRETS FOR YOU

— Chapter 7 —

Joseph, the Bible's first billionaire, has been called "the man whose dreams came true." Joseph went from pit to palace, from rags to riches. He was totally unspoiled by immense wealth when it finally came to him.

Joseph has been described as "the cultured man." Certainly he was one of the most glamorous people of ancient times. Joseph led the "jet set" of the Old Testament!

Whereas the previously described men of Genesis became millionaires, Joseph became a billionaire as second in command of the wealthiest civilization of ancient times, Egypt—overnight! (Although Joseph became an "overnight success," he spent 20 years preparing for it.)

In the process of developing a "billionaire consciousness," he developed charm, glamor, style, looks, culture, and refinement. He learned how to dress, how to entertain, and how to treat people properly. He had "flair." All of these qualities are helpful in developing a well-balanced prosperity consciousness.

In modern times, one of the world's leading billionaires recently confessed that the turning point from severe poverty to acquiring billions came for him when he bought his first tailored suit and began to associate with millionaires. By getting into their prosperous mental atmosphere, and learning from them how to dress, how to entertain and to treat people socially, he developed "flair" and style that led him to acquire millions. It is little wonder he later married one of the most famous and glamorous women of modern times. "Putting your best foot forward" is still a success secret fit for a future millionaire!

Joseph's Prosperous Background

By going to Egypt, Joseph developed his prosperity consciousness in a way he never could have, had he remained in the Land of Canaan. In Egypt he was exposed to immense wealth and all that goes with it. It is little wonder he later declared, "Ye may have meant it for evil, but God turned it to good." (Genesis 50:20)

However, Joseph was a cultured gentleman while still a shepherd in Canaan. He was taught by his father, Jacob, how to behave in the presence of princes and rulers. His good manners and education prepared him to rise quickly to a high position in Egypt.

All of the sons of Jacob had been well brought up and trained by their father, Jacob, and their grandfather, Isaac. Even as children, they had often feasted with kings and princes. The Egyptians were amazed because they had not expected these desert men to know anything about good manners.

During the course of his life, Joseph used most of the basic prosperity principles employed by the earlier millionaires of Genesis: He practiced the prosperity power of release, non-resistance, forgiveness, affirmation, picturing, recognition of God as the Source of his supply, and tithing.

Perhaps that is the reason he became a billionaire—not just a mere millionaire. In my own gradual growth out of lifelong poverty into a more abundant way of life, I have found that it is necessary to employ all of the prosperity methods that Joseph used so faithfully.

When people wail, "Those prosperity laws you write about sound good, but they do not work for me," it is because—unlike Joseph—the doubters have not practiced prosperity's dynamic techniques consistently over a period of time. That Joseph did so, and got such remarkable results, should greatly encourage you in the deliberate expansion of your own prosperity consciousness.

Specific Secrets For Gaining Enormous Wealth

What was Joseph's specific secret for manifesting such enormous wealth? Joseph's name had prosperity significance. It meant "whom Jehovah will add to." Joseph symbolizes the ability to increase substance through deliberate constructive use of one's imaging power. Joseph became a master of substance, and manifested it as vast wealth through the repeated use of one specific prosperity principle: The picturing of the mind!

Here is Joseph's greatest prosperity secret for you:
1) Through the deliberate practice of appreciating the vast wealth he saw all around him in affluent Egypt, and
2) Through picturing vast wealth for himself, Joseph became a billionaire.

From $10,000 to $100,000 A Year Income—
How She Maintained It

A businesswoman had gone from $10,000 a year financial income to $100,000 a year income after she began to make Prosperity Maps each year, placing on them the financial income she desired.

Then one year after she had reached her $100,000 goal she neglected to make another Prosperity Map picturing her continued financial success. The results? Her income began to dwindle. She was baffled and frightened about this sudden turn of events—until she realized she was no longer picturing financial success. When she made a new Prosperity Map, picturing a $100,000 a year financial income for herself, it again manifested for her. (See instructions at conclusion of this chapter for making a Prosperity Map.)

Like Abraham, the first millionaire, you should learn to manifest visible prosperity out of invisible substance, as symbolized by the barren land of Canaan. Then, like Joseph, the first billionaire, you must go a step further, and learn to manifest that invisible substance as lavish visible abundance. Going to Egypt, where he was surrounded by lavish wealth, helped Joseph to picture it for himself, and to mentally accept it. Lavish abundance is a part of a well-balanced prosperity consciousness.

Remember that Joseph symbolizes the imagination—that powerful mental faculty—that forms ideas first in the invisible substance of the universe—and then brings those ideas into visible form. *The picturing power of the mind is one of the oldest devices known to man for getting what he wants.* Joseph proved it.

As will be shown in this chapter, the experiences that Joseph went through before he gained vast wealth symbolize the discipline you must experience in order to gain vast wealth, and to maintain it.

Why You Should Keep Quiet About What You Picture

In the Land of Canaan, Joseph had been trained to be chief of the tribe and successor to his father. As such an heir, he wore a coat of many colors. This special attention from his father caused jealousy among Joseph's brothers.

When you begin to prosper, jealousy may be reflected toward you. If so, do not be surprised by it and do not respond to it. Protect yourself by declaring often, "LOVE ENVIETH NOT. THE PROSPERING TRUTH HAS SET ME FREE TO PROSPER."

Joseph dreamed of dominion when he seemed to have none. You should too, but you must keep quiet about your dreams. Joseph was clairvoyant and had some prophetic dreams, but he made the mistake of innocently telling his dreams to his jealous brothers. "His father rebuked him . . . and his brethren envied him." (Genesis 37:10, 11) His brothers retaliated by selling him into Egyptian slavery.

Joseph's dreams were a prophecy of the great events that were to happen to him later. His dreams were also a prophecy of his attainment of a superior consciousness of universal substance. When he developed that consciousness, he would become an "overnight billionaire." To that billionaire consciousness, his brothers were destined to come and ask for help. His billionaire consciousness was to save them and the entire ancient world from starvation!

How Joseph's Prosperity Consciousness Expanded In Egypt—How Yours Can Too

Ironically, Joseph's prosperity consciousness began expanding when his brothers sold him to some Arab traders who were on their way to Egypt. He was purchased for 20 shekels of silver—or between $12 and $15! It also seems ironic that his value went from about $15 to that of a billionaire after he was immersed in an atmosphere of lavish abundance, and pictured it for himself.

In Egypt, Joseph began expanding his prosperity consciousness in an outer way. Joseph had come from the barren hill country of Canaan, across the sandy desert to the lush green lands of the Nile Delta, then into the teeming city of Tarius, also known as "Zoan."

There, in that prosperous trading center of Tarius, Joseph saw for the first time every conceivable kind of merchandise: Bolts of cloth, bundles of spice, baskets of luscious fruit, beautiful objects of copper and gold.

Also, the people looked and dressed differently in Egypt. These men were cleanshaven, not bearded as were the men of Canaan. They wore cloth and linen apparel, rather than skins. The more prosperous men wore neckbands of colored metal beads. They also rode in two-wheeled, horse-drawn chariots. This was all magnificence beyond Joseph's wildest dreams.

As previously mentioned, you have to become aware of prosperity, even lavish abundance, in an outer way in order to demonstrate it in your own life. This is one of the most valuable lessons I have learned over the years.

I am certainly not in a position to compare my progress with that of the fabled Joseph. Yet I know that his prosperity methods work. When still living in one room in Alabama, I learned for the first time to bless and appreciate the wealth of the universe, and the success of other people.

As I determined to accept nothing but the best in my own life, too, this decision led me out of that one room into a more prosperous way of life. That decision led to my first mink coat, to shopping at the famous Neiman-Marcus in Texas, and later to a coveted membership in the world famous Racquet Club in Palm Springs, California, where I now reside.

The Prosperity Lessons Joseph Learned From Potiphar

In Egypt, Joseph was sold to Potiphar, a handsome well-dressed, cleanshaven man who was very important as Captain of Pharaoh's guard. As a man of such importance, he was very wealthy.

Joseph was driven away from the market place as a slave —but in one of those magnificent chariots to his new home —the elegant estate of his new master. As the overseer of Potiphar's house and estates, he became immersed in literal wealth, and the picturing power of his mind was absorbing every bit of it!

Joseph learned how to handle prosperity in an orderly way, with wisdom and good judgment, as overseer of Potiphar's estates. He was learning how to handle properly literal wealth. "The Lord was with Joseph and he became a prosperous man." (Genesis 39:2)

Like Joseph, you will probably find the most difficult experiences you have had to meet—the ones that have caused you to discipline yourself the most—in the long run proved the most valuable in the development of your character and of your prosperity consciousness.

Shortly after I was widowed and left with an infant son to support and rear alone, I "worked my way" through business school and became secretary to a Duke-and-Harvard-educated lawyer. As his private secretary, for the next 10 years I tried to keep up with his Phi Beta Kappa mentality. The training, discipline, and experience I received in how to think positively, how to handle large sums of money that were held in trust for his corporation clients, and how to meet the first important people I had ever had contact with—all proved of inestimable value later when I became a writer, lecturer, and minister with a worldwide following.

The Prospering Power of Injustice

At the height of Joseph's success, as the overseer of Potiphar's estates, injustice struck. He was wrongly accused by Potiphar's wife, and sent to prison. This apparent injustice was a test of Joseph's expanding prosperity consciousness. Instead of fighting this apparent injustice and becoming embittered by it, Joseph took control of his thinking by becoming master of his prison experience. He knew that by mastering whatever situation he found himself in, he would learn from it, and then be freed from it in due time.

The keeper of the prison liked Joseph and committed all the prisoners to his care, so that he even prospered in prison: "That which he did, Jehovah made it to prosper." (Genesis 39:23)

Joseph could have compromised with Potiphar's wife, who was in a powerful position to help or hurt him. But Joseph intuitively knew that moral compromise was not necessary. (It never is.) He became far wealthier in his own right than Potiphar's wife could ever have helped him to become.

When Joseph did not fight for what had been taken from him he was given far more later, because he had developed the prosperity consciousness which could not be taken from him.

Here is one of the billionaire secrets you learn from Joseph: Instead of fretting about what can be taken from you, you should persevere in developing a prosperity consciousness that cannot be taken from you. When you have done this, no person, thing, or event can keep that from you which the universe has for you!

The Prospering Power of Discipline

Joseph needed the quiet time that came to him in prison, away from the world, for further development of his imaging power. He needed this quiet time to gain an interior control of substance, to become non-resistant, adaptable, and flexible, so that he could continue to grow and expand.

He knew that if he became rigid and said that things had to be a certain way, he would repel the substance of the universe from manifesting for him.

Also, Joseph had learned all he could by overseeing Potiphar's prosperity. He had outgrown that experience and needed to be freed from it. The act of apparent injustice that placed him in prison was actually a step forward.

Even in the dungeon, Joseph became master of it. He knew he must master those unwanted experiences, and gain the good from them, rather than letting them master him.

When the chief servants of Pharaoh's household were imprisoned, Joseph interpreted their dreams: The royal cupbearer was restored to favor as Joseph predicted. The royal baker was hanged as Joseph had foreseen.

When the royal cupbearer's life was saved, he promised to speak to the King about Joseph's unfair imprisonment, but he did not.

Instead of reacting to this further injustice, Joseph kept right on nonresistantly gaining control of his prison experiences. He kept on picturing better than the best he was then experiencing. If he had fought back, he would have dissipated his expanding prosperity consciousness. He would have had to start all over again in gathering universal substance together in the invisible and then in the visible realms. He would have had to start all over again in picturing it. *There is prospering power in not fighting back!*

Two Secrets For Getting Results Through Picturing

Joseph knew these secrets for getting results through picturing:

First: You draw the substance of the universe into definite form in the visible world through your definite pictures.

Second: If you hold on peacefully and confidently to what you are picturing, you will manifest it as visible results in your life. But if you get angry and resentful then universal substance evaporates, and you have to start all over again.

In the face of all this injustice, Joseph "kept his cool" because he knew he was being disciplined for greater things! One day, 2 years later, his nonresistance paid off. Pharaoh had a dream that all the wise men of Egypt could not interpret.

Suddenly the cupbearer to the King remembered Joseph. He was brought out of the dungeon. He interpreted the dreams as a prophecy of the 7 years of plenty, and the 7 years of famine that were coming to Egypt.

At this point, Joseph's troubles were over. A long period of severe discipline was ended, but it had been worth it.

Life As A Billionaire

One day Joseph had been a forgotten prisoner, a slave. The next day he was Prime Minister of Egypt, the second richest man in the ancient world! Only King Pharaoh was wealthier.

Some of the manifestations of lavish abundance, which the picturing power of the mind provided for Joseph, were these:

King Pharaoh placed on Joseph's finger a signet ring as a symbol of royal authority and vast wealth. Joseph was clothed in embroidered garments. A gold chain was placed around his neck. He was given Pharaoh's second chariot for his own. He was given a lovely Egyptian wife, the daughter of a highly respected priest. Pharaoh conferred upon him an Egyptian title which was to be prophetic. It meant "Saviour of the world. " Pharaoh said grandly, "I have set thee over all the land of Egypt." (Genesis 41:41) The King meant by this statement, "I have set thee over the wealth of the universe," because the great empire of Egypt was the richest country of the ancient world.

Such wealth and honor would have turned the head of the average person. It would have emotionally unbalanced most people, but not Joseph, who had spent years being disciplined and prepared for the enormous wealth that was suddenly poured out upon him.

The Prospering Power of Forgiveness

Joseph's positive attitude about what he had been through is shown in the way he named his sons:

His first son was named "Manasseh" meaning "forgetfulness." Joseph explained, "God has made me forget all my hardships." (Genesis 41:51)

His second son was named "Ephraim" meaning "fruitful." Joseph said, "God has made me fruitful in the land of my affliction." (Genesis 41:52)

In these 2 statements, Joseph was practicing the prospering power of forgiveness. When you, too, say of hard experiences and difficult people, "I PRONOUNCE YOU GOOD," you open the way to reap the vast benefits of the prospering power of forgiveness.

A businessman in Palm Springs, California said, "I know that forgiveness prospers. A number of customers had not paid their bills. After the usual methods of attempted collection, I decided to try forgiveness. I took off a week and vacationed at Newport Beach. I spent a great deal of time reading along inspirational lines, and practicing forgiveness. I wrote out the names of those owing me money on my 'forgiveness list.' I called their names daily and declared that all things were cleared up between us. It worked! When I returned to my office, several of the largest outstanding accounts had been paid while I was away."

Lavish Abundance During 7 Years of Plenty

Then came 7 years of abundance: "In the 7 plenteous years, the earth brought forth by handfuls." (Genesis 41:47) 47)

During this period, Joseph displayed great humility. He did not sit back idly amid his vast wealth, but he worked diligently as an able administrator. "Joseph went out over the land of Egypt." (Genesis 41:45) He had not been emotionally unbalanced by vast wealth.

During this period, he lived and worked amid unlimited abundance. "Joseph stored up grain in vast abundance, like the sand of the seas, until he ceased to measure it, for it could not be measured." (Genesis 41:49)

As Prime Minister he had a marvelous life, even though he worked steadily. He entertained in his home and at public banquets. He lived like a king. As a celebrity in his own right, he was loved everywhere.

It was all the result of years of disciplining his thinking, of picturing the good, and of not fighting back. Joseph proved that the longer your good is in coming, the bigger it will be when it comes, if you persist in expecting it, and in preparing to receive it.

The Riches That A Famine Brought

During the following 7 years of famine, Joseph's family came from the Land of Canaan begging for food. When his big chance for revenge came, Joseph ignored it by forgiving his family, his former tormenters who had tried to destroy him.

He explained, "It all happened according to God's plan. God set me ahead of you, so that I might save you from hunger." (Genesis 45:7) He gave them gold, clothing, wagons, donkeys, and fertile, well-watered grassland in the green Delta region of Egypt in which to live. He prosperously affirmed, "I will give you the good of the land. Ye shall eat the fat of the land." (Genesis 45:18)

King Pharaoh was also generous to Joseph's family: "The land of Egypt is before you." (Genesis 47:6) Joseph's father, Jacob, had already become a millionaire, as evidenced by the vast flocks and possessions he brought with him to Egypt. Due to Joseph's generosity, coupled with that of the powerful King Pharaoh, the rest of Joseph's family became very rich, too.

Joseph brought Egypt safely through the famine and lived with his family there in honor, esteem, and vast wealth to a ripe old age. He promised his kinsmen that God would one day take them out of Egypt into their own rich Promised Land.

Yet there was a divine purpose in their following him to Egypt. There the Hebrews came into contact with an advanced civilization, and they developed the national prosperity consciousness they would need and use later to become one of the wealthiest groups of people the world has ever known!

The Prosperous Power of Giving—and Of Giving Thanks

Although nothing is said in the Book of Genesis about Joseph tithing, he did so because his father, grandfather, and great grandfather before him had tithed. It was a Hebrew tradition.

Also, Joseph felt so strongly about the prospering power of tithing that he made a law over all Egypt that the people must give 1/5 or 2/10's of everything to Pharaoh, who in turn supported the temples and priests. Thus, the prosperous-minded Joseph required them to tithe not just one-tenth, but two!

In the life of Joseph is found a constant recognition of God as the Source of his supply and vast success. There are numerous Biblical references pointing this out, such as:

"The God of your Father hath given you the treasure." (Genesis 43:23) "Jehovah was with Joseph and he was a prosperous man." (Genesis 39:2) "The blessing of Jehovah was upon all that he had in the house and in the field." (Genesis 39:5)

On the way to Egypt to live, Joseph's father had stopped at Beersheba in the land of Canaan to offer sacrifices. This would indicate that he followed the ancient custom of giving "thank offerings" and tithe offerings in appreciation for:

1) Joseph's safety in Egypt and his success there. 2) In appreciation for the family being saved from starvation. 3) In appreciation for their reunion in Egypt.

The wealthy Jacob had long since learned that to give a "faith offering" before his prayers were answered as-

sured results; and to give afterwards sealed and protected
the results and made them permanent. No wonder he lived
amid such lavish abundance in his later years in Egypt. He
had earned it in consciousness through his faithful giving
over the years.

The Greatest Prosperity Secret of All

The greatest prosperity secret that we learn from Joseph
is this:

*Vast wealth did not come to Joseph until he was ready
for it mentally and emotionally.* After the depths of humiliation — which he never accepted — Joseph was then
lifted up into high honor and vast wealth. It did not turn
his head, because he had earned it in consciousness first. He
was ready to accept it and to retain it.

As symbolized by the events of his life, Joseph developed
a superior consciousness of universal substance. He learned
how to manifest that universal substance as visible wealth
for himself and for the entire ancient world, mainly through
the picturing power of the mind.

A Billionaire Meditation

The following statements, paraphrased from the life of
Joseph, can help you develop a billionaire consciousness:

" 'PUTTING YOUR BEST FOOT FORWARD' IS
STILL A SUCCESS SECRET FIT FOR A BILLION-
AIRE! JOSEPH BECAME A MASTER OF SUBSTANCE
AND MANIFESTED IT AS VAST WEALTH
THROUGH THE REPEATED USE OF THE PICTUR-
ING POWER OF THE MIND. I DO TOO! LAVISH
ABUNDANCE IS PART OF A WELL-BALANCED

PROSPERITY CONSCIOUSNESS. THE PICTURING POWER OF THE MIND IS THE OLDEST DEVICE KNOWN TO MAN FOR GETTING WHAT HE WANTS. I USE IT DAILY.

"I KEEP QUIET ABOUT WHAT I AM PICTURING. LOVE ENVIETH NOT. THE PROSPERING TRUTH HAS SET ME FREE TO PROSPER. I AM MASTER OF SUBSTANCE. AS I ATTAIN A SUPERIOR CONSCIOUSNESS OF UNIVERSAL SUBSTANCE, I PROSPER EXCEEDINGLY. I DARE TO EXPAND MY PROSPERITY CONSCIOUSNESS IN OUTER, AS WELL AS INNER, WAYS. I LEARN HOW TO HANDLE PROSPERITY IN AN ORDERLY WAY WITH WISDOM AND GOOD JUDGMENT. INSTEAD OF FRETTING ABOUT WHAT CAN BE TAKEN AWAY FROM ME, I PERSEVERE IN DEVELOPING A PROSPEROUS STATE OF MIND THAT CANNOT BE TAKEN FROM ME. I GAIN AN INTERIOR CONTROL OF SUBSTANCE BY BECOMING NONRESISTANT, ADAPTABLE, FLEXIBLE. I AM NOT RIGID OR NEGATIVE, SO I DO NOT REPEL SUBSTANCE. INSTEAD OF REACTING TO ANY APPARENT INJUSTICE, I CONSTANTLY PICTURE BETTER THAN THE BEST THAT I AM NOW EXPERIENCING. I PROVE THAT THERE IS PROSPERING POWER IN NOT FIGHTING BACK.

"I KEEP MY COOL BECAUSE I KNOW I AM BEING DISCIPLINED FOR GREATER THINGS. WHEN WEALTH AND HONOR COME, THEY DO NOT UNBALANCE ME. I PRACTICE THE PROSPERING POWER OF FORGIVENESS BY PRONOUNCING ALL OF MY EXPERIENCES GOOD. I DISPLAY GREAT

HUMILITY. I CONSTANTLY RECOGNIZE GOD AS
THE SOURCE OF MY VAST AND EVER-INCREAS-
ING SUPPLY. I TITHE MY WAY TO VAST WEALTH.
I PROTECT MY WEALTH AND MAKE IT PERMA-
NENT THROUGH MY 'FAITH OFFERINGS,'
'THANK OFFERINGS,' AND CONSISTENT TITHES
TO GOD'S WORK. AS I DO THESE THINGS, I
KNOW THAT VAST WEALTH COMES TO ME JUST
AS SOON AS I AM READY FOR IT MENTALLY
AND EMOTIONALLY. THEREFORE, IT DOES NOT
TURN MY HEAD BECAUSE I HAVE EARNED IT IN
CONSCIOUSNESS. KNOWING THIS, I REJOICE
AND ENJOY THE WEALTH OF THE UNIVERSE AS
IT FLOWS TO ME UNCEASINGLY."

INSTRUCTIONS FOR MAKING A PROSPERITY
MAP OR WHEEL OF FORTUNE

How To Picture Your Good

The fantastic power that lies in deliberately picturing
what you want was brought to my attention many years
ago by an engineer in Alabama who designed a "wheel of
fortune" which worked so well for him that he went from
a mediocre job in the Deep South to a multimillion dollar
construction job in the Midwest.

He used a large piece of poster board, outlined a circle on
it which he divided for the various departments of his life:

THE FIRST BILLIONAIRE, JOSEPH

Financial, job, family, health, vacation, spiritual growth. In each segment he placed pictures of the good he wished to experience in that phase of his life.

More recently, a college professor in Austin, Texas, and a lawyer in San Antonio have shown me simpler "success maps" which they have made that produced equally successful results for them.

Also, from years of experience in making success maps for myself and others, I would like to share with you these ideas, which I have found very helpful in manifesting one's good through pictures:

First: Keep quiet about your pictures. Do not discuss them or try to convince others to try this method. The words "secret" and "sacred" have the same root meaning. What is sacred should be secret.

Second: Use big, beautiful, colorful poster boards, if you want big, beautiful, colorful results in your life.

A college professor made a small, crowded, drab, colorless success map for travel abroad and it worked. He had a crowded, drab, colorless trip.

Third: Use definite colors for definite results desired. According to the ancient science of color, you should use:

Green or gold poster boards for financial success maps, for job and career success.

Yellow or white for increased spiritual understanding.

Blue for intellectual accomplishments such as writing a book, or finishing a degree.

Orange or bright yellow for health, energy, a more vital life.

Pink, rose or warm red for love, harmony, marriage, happiness in human relationships.

Color is important because color impresses the subconscious mind much faster than black or white.

Whether or not you follow the foregoing ancient color chart, be sure to use colored poster board, always in a color that appeals to you emotionally.

Fourth: Use colored pictures, rather than black and white ones, on your colored poster boards. A recent comment was "Now I know why my pictured good took so long to manifest. I had used black and white pictures and backgrounds rather than colored ones."

Fifth: Do not clutter your board, unless you want cluttered results. Make several maps for various phases of your life.

A housewife recently exclaimed, "Now I know why our house is so crowded. We placed a small, crowded house on our success map and we got just that!" Soon after she made a new map for a larger house, it came through her husband's promotion and job transfer.

Sixth: On your financial poster board, put money, not just things you want. Otherwise you may get those "things" plus indebtedness! Use play money or checks.

Also use specific affirmations for wealth if you expect specific financial increase, such as the following:

"I AM OPEN AND RECEPTIVE TO THE VAST WEALTH THAT THE UNIVERSE HAS FOR ME NOW. I AM BEAUTIFULLY AND APPROPRIATELY CLOTHED, HOUSED, TRANSPORTED AND SUPPLIED WITH THE RICH SUBSTANCE OF THE UNIVERSE NOW. THE ENORMOUS SUMS OF MONEY THAT ARE MINE BY DIVINE RIGHT NOW MANIFEST FOR ME, UNDER GRACE IN PERFECT WAYS. I WELCOME THEM IN HUMILITY, WISDOM AND

PEACE NOW. I AM RECEIVING, I AM RECEIVING NOW, I AM RECEIVING ALL THE WEALTH THAT THE UNIVERSE HAS FOR ME NOW."

A specific affirmation for marriage that has worked for a number of people after they placed it on their success map was this:

"THE CHRIST MIND ACTIVE IN ME NOW MANIFESTS FOR ME MY OWN TRUE (WIFE, HUSBAND) FOR LIFE. WE ENJOY A HEALTHY, HAPPY, PROSPEROUS MARRIAGE TOGETHER HERE AND NOW."

Seventh: Place a spiritual symbol on your poster board, such as a picture of the Christ or the Bible. This gives your desires a spiritual protection, and opens the way for what you have pictured or something better to come to you.

Eighth: View your success map every day, preferably early in the morning and just before sleeping. The more often you view your pictured desires, the quicker the results will come.

A young insurance salesman sold more than a million dollar's worth of insurance during his first year in business after he quietly followed the foregoing instructions and pictured those results on a success map.

SUMMARY

1. Joseph symbolizes the ability to manifest substance as tangible results through the picturing power of the mind. He has been called "the man whose dreams came true." Ours can too when we employ his methods.

2. Joseph dreamed of dominion when he seemed to have none, but he innocently told his dreams to his jealous brothers who sold him into Egyptian slavery. From Joseph we learn to keep quiet about what we are picturing, but also to keep picturing it.

3. Like Joseph in Egypt, we must become aware of prosperity in outer ways in order to manifest it.

4. Like Joseph in Potiphar's house, we must learn how to handle large sums with wisdom.

5. Joseph's imprisonment was a test of his expanding prosperity consciousness. He became master of substance, even in prison. He was being disciplined for greater things through that period of apparent tests.

6. The longer Joseph's good was in coming, the bigger it was when it came. Joseph was not unbalanced by sudden wealth because he had spent years being disciplined and prepared inwardly for it.

7. Joseph made three statements after he became Prime Minister showing forgiveness of his family, all of which are marvelous decrees for us to use too in the face of apparent injustice:

   1) "GOD HAS MADE ME FORGET ALL MY HARDSHIPS."

   2) "GOD HAS MADE ME FRUITFUL IN THE LAND OF MY AFFLICTION."

   3) "YE MAY HAVE MEANT IT FOR EVIL, BUT GOD TURNED IT TO GOOD."

8. A national prosperity consciousness was developed by the Hebrews in Egypt, which they would need later. There they were exposed to immense wealth.

9. Vast wealth, esteem, honor did not come to Joseph until he was ready for them, mentally and emotionally.

10. Joseph continued to work diligently in Egypt while enjoying the privilege of vast wealth.

11. Joseph's name had prosperity significance. It meant "whom Jehovah will add to."

12. Enormous wealth and honor came to Joseph through his quiet, persistent use of the picturing power of the mind. As second in command of the wealthiest civilization of ancient times, he became the Bible's first billionaire.

THE FIRST MILLIONAIRESS--
RUTH

HER PROSPERITY SECRETS FOR YOU

— Chapter 8 —

The Book of Ruth, best known as a love story, is also one of the greatest prosperity stories of all times!

It is a master short story containing human interest, tragedy, humor, love, and a very happy ending. It brings a message of hope to those people who have suffered from sorrow and loss, and who want to see their good restored. As this story proves, *there are always returning cycles, when the good that seemed lost returns again in a new guise.*

Although the famous love story of Ruth is not found in the Book of Genesis, it is being included in this study of the Bible's early millionaires for 2 reasons:

First: The historical setting of the Book of Ruth is uncertain. Although it follows the story of the Judges in the Bible, many historians feel it was written during an earlier era.

Second: It seems appropriate to place Ruth in importance with the millionaires of Genesis, because she became the Bible's first millionairess through her own actions.

Though the wives of Abraham, Isaac, Jacob, and Joseph enjoyed the immense wealth accumulated by their husbands, Ruth was the first among the early Bible women to show through the actions of her life (and through those of her mother-in-law) the mental steps that were taken to manifest the lavish abundance she later enjoyed.

(Eve of the Creation Story in Genesis 1 and 2 was "the allegorical millionairess," symbolizing every person's feeling nature. However, she is being given only "honorable mention" here because Eve misused her feelings by dwelling upon a belief in lack, in the midst of abundance. Whereas, Eve started out rich and ended up poor, Ruth did just the opposite: She was poor in the beginning but grew out of poverty into tremendous wealth. We can, too, as we follow her mystical success formulas.)

Although Ruth attracted wealth in a traditional way—by landing a rich husband—her actions symbolize the use of some basic prosperity principles that you can use to manifest increased abundance in your life, too.

By interpreting the mental steps Ruth and Naomi took, you gain a quick review of the basic laws of prosperity that were used by all of the early millionaires. Thus her story is a fitting one to conclude this study of the ancient millionaires, and their deliberate use of universal success principles.

Prosperity Begins In Bethlehem

Her prosperity story begins in Bethlehem not with Ruth but with her future mother-in-law, Naomi. This woman and her husband left Bethlehem because of a famine there. They went into the Land of Moab. Hardship and sorrow followed when Naomi's husband and 2 sons died there, leaving her destitute.

Actually Naomi's hardships began when she left Bethlehem, which means "house of bread." Bethlehem is symbolic of that state of mind in which man realizes that Divine Substance is the one and only reality in his financial affairs, regardless of the appearances of the moment.

When an apparent famine or lack arises, man in a prosperous Bethlehem state of mind knows what to do: He affirms that Divine Substance is mightily at work for him, manifesting increased supply for him in rich appropriate form. He does not panic over the temporary appearance of lack.

Naomi did not do this. Instead she panicked over the appearance of poverty and left Bethlehem, thereby leaving a prosperous state of mind.

Lack Always Manifests In The Land of Moab

Naomi went off to the Land of Moab expecting to be prospered there, but she only met with more hardships. Naomi symbolizes every person who learns about the power of prosperous thinking, yet in times of distress, does not use it. She symbolizes those people, who in the face of lack, try to find an easy way out by going off to the Land of Moab.

Moab symbolizes that material state of mind that says,

"I do not know how to solve this problem of lack and distress in an inner way, so I will go back to my former methods of fixing things up in some outer way." But when Naomi tried to ""fix things up" in an outward way, she just encountered more lack and loss.

You must learn to think things through rather than trying to force things through. When you deliberately employ prosperous thinking, your prosperity thoughts move on the lavish substance of the universe, manifesting it as rich ideas, and as increased supply in your life in any number of ways. Your prosperous thinking develops the rich state of mind known as Bethlehem.

When you try to force things through in an outer way and panic at every sign of lack, your hardships just multiply. This develops the limited "hardship consciousness" known as Moab.

How A Widow Happily Remarried After Leaving Moab

A widow of ten years wished to remarry and lead a happier, more normal way of life. She had prayed, affirmed, and pictured a happy new marriage for several years but nothing happened.

She finally realized that she needed to move out of the area where she had overcome tremendous hardships—both financial and in her family life. She began to declare, "I NOW MOVE FORWARD INTO MY EXPANDED GOOD, DIVINELY DIRECTED AND LAVISHLY PROSPERED. I NOW MOVE FORWARD INTO MY PROMISED LAND, WHERE I BELONG."

Soon a job offer came to her from a nearby city. She took it, then she released furniture, clothing, even friends that were connected with the barren widowed-way-of-life she had led for so long.

In her new surroundings, she moved into a beautiful new furnished apartment. New friends opened a busy social life to her. Within the year she had met and married a very fine man—whom she would never have met and married had she remained in her former surroundings. They soon settled in their own new home, surrounded by new possessions, and an expanded way of life. But in spite of all of her former years of praying for a new life, nothing had happened until she first got out of a former Moab-hardship-state of mind, and released all that went with it.

The Prosperity Lesson That Naomi Learned

Naomi finally came to her senses and returned to Bethlehem, where she got into a prosperous state of mind and met her problems successfully.

She learned what we all must learn: That *once you know how to use the power of thought constructively, no other method works for solving your problems.* If you try to revert to the former methods of rushing around, trying to make things right in some outward way, the situation only gets worse. It never gets better until you return to Bethlehem, or begin to use the inner laws of prosperity again.

You can quickly return to Bethlehem and reap the prosperous benefits of that rich state of mind:

First: By affirming that you do not depend upon persons or conditions for your prosperity; that God is the Source of your prosperity, and that God provides His own amazing channels of supply to you now.

Second: By declaring that Divine Substance (the mystics called it "the body of God") is the one and only reality in your financial affairs; and that Divine Substance is manifesting in rich appropriate form for you now.

How A Teacher Demonstrated Prosperity For Self and Others

Does it work in a practical way to do this? A teacher from New Hampshire recently wrote: " 'DIVINE SUBSTANCE IS THE ONE AND ONLY REALITY.' I am happy to say that shortly after I started to declare these words every day, I obtained 2 new art students, I obtained an order for the product I sell, and I received the inspiration for a children's book.

"As I used the statement 'DIVINE SUBSTANCE APPROPRIATELY MANIFESTS FOR ME HERE AND NOW' I had several other prosperous results. I gave my brother, a businessman, these statements to use and he has already had 3 prosperity demonstrations!"

Physical Form Is The Lowest Form of Energy

Why can't you continue to use outer physical force, instead of the inner mental and spiritual forces, to try to solve your problems?

Because *physical force is the lowest form of energy, while mental and spiritual forces release the highest form of energy.* Once you learn how to release the highest form of en-

ergy and power into a situation, the lower weaker forms of
energy do not respond to you anymore. Physical energy is
a slowed-down vibration that has limited power in the midst
of accelerated mental and spiritual vibrations. Physical energy is meant to be a vehicle through which high-powered
mental and spiritual energy expresses. Physical power is not
an end in itself.

When you revert to outer material methods because it
seems difficult to work out your problems through use of
inner mental and spiritual methods, the result is always dis-
astrous. Either temporary results, confusion, or hard experiences follow.

Knowledge carries sacred responsibility. You do not learn
about the power of prosperous thinking until you are ready
in your soul growth to begin using it. Once you are given
this valuable knowledge, you must use it for your continued
growth and expansion. If you do not, the result is always sad
and unproductive.

How A Businessman Got Out of Moab and Made $75,000

A businessman started tithing at a time when his tithe
check amounted to only $10 a month. He prospered so much
that his tithe check was soon $100 a month. He then rea-
soned that $100 a month was "too much" to give away, so
he stopped tithing, and returned to the hard-work consciousness known as Moab. Disaster followed. He was brought
down to poverty and humiliation through business reverses.

He finally realized his foolish mistake, and returned to a
Bethlehem state of mind by beginning to tithe again. Later
he was making $75,000.00 a year and gladly tithed $7500.00.
He had learned his prosperity lesson well.

What had happened? By putting God first financially in the beginning, he had gotten into the prosperous Bethlehem state of mind, where his tithes went from $10 to $100 a month. But when he reasoned that a $100-a-month tithe was "too much" and stopped giving it, he reverted to a Moab state of mind and reaped according to that hardship consciousness. By reverting to a limited way of thinking, limited results naturally followed.

Whenever you revert to material methods because it seems difficult to work out your problems from a higher level, the result is always disappointing. *You cannot go backwards, you must go forward, in order to succeed in life.*

How To Pay The Bills and Taxes, Get A Home Or Job, Sell Property or Get Efficient Employees

In the Bethlehem state of mind, prosperity and every other blessing, is added. The riches that come through the deliberate use of prosperous thinking are permanent, because they are not confined to your outer affairs, but express through every department of your life, both inward and outward.

There is a practical way you can get out of Moab into the abundant state of mind known as Bethlehem: By declaring often that you do not depend upon persons or conditions, but that God is the Source of your supply and provides His own amazing channels of supply to you now.

Do you realize the practical power there is in doing this? When there are bills to pay, clothing to purchase, income tax payments to meet, that is the time to declare that in all these situations, God is the Source of your supply.

If there is property to rent, that is the time to realize that God is the Source, and that His Divine Love is providing just the right tenants for you now. If there is property to sell, that is the time to realize that since God is the Source, He can draw to you the ones who are looking for such property, and who will be blessed by it.

If there is a need for a home, that is the time to realize that God is the Source of the perfect place for you to live, that in the Father's house are many mansions.

If there is a need for a job, that is the time to realize that God is the Source of all opportunity, so He has just the right place of service awaiting you.

If there is a need for more workers, that is the time to realize that God is the Source of all work and all workers. Declare that you are trusting Him to provide everything that is necessary to the expression of a good life.

How Army Officer And Businessman Prospered

A businessman said he became a branch manager for his company after he began to declare daily: "I LOOK TO GOD FOR GUIDANCE AND SUPPLY." Another man found work, though he was past retirement age, after he daily declared: "I LOOK TO GOD FOR GUIDANCE AND SUPPLY. I AM NOW GUIDED INTO MY TRUE PLACE WITH THE TRUE PEOPLE AND WITH THE TRUE PROSPERITY."

An Army officer said he and his wife always found just the right home for their family near crowded military bases by declaring: "I DAILY LOOK TO GOD FOR GUIDANCE AND SUPPLY. I AM BEAUTIFULLY AND AP-

PROPRIATELY HOUSED WITH THE RICH SUB-STANCE OF GOD NOW."

How To Develop "A Millionaire Consciousness"

Naomi had to return to a Bethlehem state of mind in order to demonstrate prosperity, and so must we. Since the word "Bethlehem" means "house of substance," you can get into a prosperous state of mind and reap its vast benefits by quietly inviting the substance of the universe into your life: "I INVITE THE POWERFUL LOVING SUBSTANCE OF THE UNIVERSE INTO MY FINANCIAL AFFAIRS NOW. I INVITE THE POWERFUL LOVING SUBSTANCE OF THE UNIVERSE TO MANIFEST WEALTH AND ABUNDANCE FOR ME NOW, QUICKLY AND IN PEACE."

How Several Thousand Dollars Came To Me

Does this simple technique work? I was once startled at how quickly it worked for me. One afternoon I meditated for a long time on the powerful loving substance of the universe, and invited it into my life. That night a friend paid a visit and handed me a check for several thousand dollars. It was a "love offering" in appreciation for some ideas in one of my books which had prospered this friend. The check to me was a tithe from that prosperity demonstration. In gratitude, I gave thanks for the quick way that universal substance had heard my call and had responded.

How Businesswoman Became A Millionaire

A businesswoman quietly went from limited financial circumstances to a life of affluent financial independence (she became a millionaire), after she began to spend time daily meditating upon the rich substance of the universe, and inviting it to manifest lavish abundance for her.

The "millionaire meditation method" which she developed and suggests is this:

Get by yourself for a few minutes every day. Release your worries, relax your body, and quietly invite the rich substance of the universe to flow into your mind, body, and affairs. State that this rich universal substance is providing you with whatever you need for your growth and expansion. It might be health, guidance, specific ideas or information, a job, more money, peace of mind, more leisure and time for reflection, or more harmonious relationships.

Do not try to force this Power to do anything for you. To try to compel it only repels it. Be relaxed, receptive, open minded, humble. Do not get impatient, but practice this simple asking and inviting method daily. Something wonderful will happen, if you persevere!

How A Housewife Demonstrated Financial Independence

A housewife had long suffered from privation, because her husband was one of those people whose theme song was, "We can't afford it." Upon learning about the power of prosperous thinking, this housewife was relieved to learn that God, not her husband, was the Source of her supply. She began quietly to invite the wealth of the universe into her life every day. That universal wealth quickly responded!

She soon learned that she had become an heir to a family business. Her husband scoffed at her inheritance, since it was a business that had never prospered. In spite of this, she began quietly to invite that same universal wealth to take control of her inheritance.

The heirs placed this business under new management, and it began to produce as never before! This quiet prayerful lady was soon receiving substantial monthly income checks from this business. She blossomed forth with a mink jacket, diamond rings, a redecorated house— all the beauty she had secretly longed for over the years.

Her husband (still in a Moab consciousness) continued to say, "We cannot afford it." His wife's answer? From her prosperous Bethlehem consciousness she replied, "Maybe you can't, honey, but I *can* because I have finally learned that God is the Source of my supply." This housewife discovered that when you invite the rich substance of the universe into your life, remarkable things *do* happen!

Prosperous Reasons Why Ruth Went To Bethlehem

Naomi had 2 daughters-in-law. One was Ruth, the other was Orpah. When Naomi returned to Bethlehem, she took Ruth with her, but left Orpah in the Land of Moab, and rightly so. "Orpah" symbolizes a material state of mind, one that loves that which can be seen outwardly.

Ruth loved the inner world of mind and Spirit. She symbolizes *one who holds fast to the power of prosperous thinking until it has had time to manifest permanent results in one's life.* (This, of course, is the secret of permanent success.)

Experts have estimated that success results 98% from inner work (Ruth), and 2% from outer action (Orpah). Since Ruth persisted in doing this inner work, even in the midst of the most trying circumstances, it was appropriate that she should have accompanied Naomi to Bethlehem.

Gathering Your Good Bit By Bit Leads To Wealth

When Ruth and Naomi arrived in Bethlehem, they had nothing. Naomi was bitter about their poverty, because she was still judging according to appearances. But Ruth knew this was the test. She uncomplainingly did the things that lay at hand to do, while practicing prosperous thinking.

One thing she could do to meet their immediate needs was to go into the harvest fields as a gleaner. The word "glean" means "to collect gradually," or "to collect bit by bit." Ruth collected bit by bit the grain that was left by the reapers. Granting this privilege was one of the ways the Hebrews helped their poor people.

When you have a need, you must be willing to do the same thing: Practice thinking prosperously, and gather the prosperous results bit by bit, if necessary. *As you quietly and uncomplainingly collect your good bit by bit, it increases.*

From One Room In Alabama To Famed Actor's Former Home In California

I started writing about the inner laws of prosperity at a time when I was living in one room. I felt ridiculous telling other people how to be prospered, while I was still living in only one room. But I realized that I had to expand my prosperity consciousness in order to break out of such a narrow world, and that the best way to expand was by thinking, affirming, teaching, and writing about abundance.

A gleaner is one who collects his good gradually, if necessary. I found that the only way to get out of that one room was "bit by bit." As I quietly blessed it, beautified it, and lived as prosperously as possible in it, it became easier to picture something better. That method worked.

I moved from that one room into a beautiful new church manse in Alabama. It was not mine, but living in it was a step forward. Later I lived in a series of apartments in Austin, Texas. Each was nicer than the previous one, as I blessed each one and fixed it up "bit by bit."

This method led me to my first home in San Antonio, Texas—a Mexican hacienda which I filled with custom-made furnishings from Mexico. Later in Palm Springs, California, I bought and redecorated a larger home that had once been owned by a famous show business personality. But none of these blessings came to me suddenly, or all at once. They came "bit by bit" as I persisted.

How Ruth Became The First Millionairess

There is an axiom: *You become what you want to be by affirming that you already are!* To think prosperity, affirm prosperity, talk prosperity, and act prosperously opens the way for prosperity to appear in your life, bit by bit.

This method worked for Ruth. While she quietly and uncomplainingly gathered grain in the harvest fields, bit by bit, she was "discovered" by the millionaire owner of the field, Boaz. He was a kind, respected, wealthy citizen of Bethlehem. In her humble, receptive, uncomplaining state of mind, Ruth had unconsciously been guided to one of the richest harvest fields in Bethlehem!

The Prospering Power of Blessing

This Bethlehem millionaire, Boaz, symbolized prosperity at its best. He had become a wealthy citizen because he used some basic prosperity principles:

First: He recognized God as the Source of his supply.

Second: He knew the power of blessing God, people, substance. When he met Ruth he blessed her with the prosperous words: "A full reward will be given thee of the Lord God of Israel, under whose wings thou art come to trust." (Ruth 2:12)

He and his workers spoke words of blessing to each other in the barley fields. He said to the reapers, "The Lord be with you." They happily replied, "The Lord bless you." (Ruth 2:4) Theirs was a pleasant, prosperous relationship. No wonder Boaz was so rich! As he blessed people and things, this caused a quickening of substance which resulted in his increased wealth.

First: *Bless all that you have.* Blessing your money stamps it with increase. A dollar which has been blessed is capable of bringing you much greater good than the dollar which has not been blessed. When the word of blessing is placed upon tangible objects, those objects are surrounded with the quickening power of increase: "I BLESS ALL THAT I HAVE, AND I LOOK WITH WONDER AT ITS INCREASE NOW."

Second: *Bless all that you hope to have.* Not only should you bless what you have, but you should go a step further and bless what you would like to have. Make a list of your desires. Bless them. Invite them to come into your life. A simple word of blessing poured out upon what you have—

and upon that which you would like to have—will begin to release the superabundance of the universe to you! Declare often, "I BLESS ALL THAT I HAVE, AND ALL THAT I HOPE TO HAVE NOW."

Third: Bless people, things, or events of the past or present which have seemed to hurt you. This is another form of blessing that is all powerful. There is great prospering power in the word of blessing directed toward those people, things, or events which have hurt and disappointed you. As you practice blessing the people who have injured you, and the failures that have burdened you, an unlimited blessing can still come out of it all! Declare often, "I BLESS THOSE PEOPLE, THINGS OR EVENTS WHICH SEEMED TO HAVE HURT ME. I BLESS THE FAILURES THAT SEEMED TO HAVE BURDENED ME. I GIVE THANKS THAT A BLESSING IS NOW COMING OUT OF IT ALL."

The Prospering Power of Getting Specific

After getting into a prosperous Bethlehem state of mind, Naomi then did what we all must next do to demonstrate prosperity. She got specific.

Naomi realized that Ruth and Boaz had become interested in each other, and that she must do something about it. Ruth was a poor widow, a gleaner in the fields, whereas Boaz was the rich owner. Naomi knew she must find a way to bridge the gap between them.

She found it quickly by remembering that Boaz was a distant relative of hers. According to Hebrew law, a widow, when she remarried, was supposed to marry a relative of her late husband's family in order to protect the family name, and to retain family property.

Naomi got specific when she sent Ruth to Boaz to remind him of his family duty, and asked his protection in marriage. Her method worked. Boaz followed through according to Hebrew tradition and married Ruth. But then he would, because remember that Boaz means "prosperity at its best." Through this marriage, both Ruth and Naomi had demonstrated just that!

The Prospering Power of Sorrow

Like Naomi, when you return to the prosperous state of mind known as Bethlehem, and then get specific about what you want, your former bitterness turns to joy. *Prosperous thinking is always the victor, never the victim, when it is persistently used.*

Why was Naomi able to demonstrate so much happiness and wealth for herself and for Ruth—after a lifetime of hardships? Because she had been through so much. *Sorrow expands your consciousness tremendously.* A person who experiences sorrow in the knowledge that something good will come from the experience, expands his consciousness to such an extent that he is able to receive more good than ever before!

If sorrow seeks you out, do not shun it, because the experience of sorrow can get you ready to receive in a much bigger way than ever before! As you meet it nonresistantly, sorrow makes you let go, and release the limitations of the past. Sorrow frees your good to expand.

The Persian philosopher, Kahlil Gibran, explained it in his famous book, *The Prophet*:*

"Pain is the breaking of the shell that encloses your understanding."

Their Happy Ending Can Be Yours Too!

With Ruth's marriage to the fabulous Boaz, Naomi's former bitterness turned to joy. Although she and her daughter-in-law had returned to Bethlehem poverty stricken, they were now 2 of the richest women in the city!

Later when Ruth and Boaz gave birth to a son—who became an ancestor of Jesus, and grandfather of the illustrious King David—Naomi moved into their home, adopted their son as her own, and "lived happily ever after" as the matriarch of this rich and honorable family.

I have faith that as you use the prosperity formulas found in this chapter, and throughout this book, you too shall demonstrate a Boaz in your life—prosperity at its best.

You can begin demonstrating prosperity at its best by declaring often, "I REJOICE, BECAUSE I AM NOW EXPERIENCING PROSPERITY AT ITS BEST."

The Psalmist might have later been describing the happy ending to Ruth and Naomi's experiences—the happiness we can all experience when we follow their mystical formulas for success:

"He that goes forth and weepeth, bearing seed for sowing, shall doubtless come home with shouts of joy, bringing his sheaves with him."

(Psalms 126:6)

---

*THE PROPHET by Kahlil Gibran, copyrighted 1923, was published by Alfred A. Knopf, New York, N.Y.

SUMMARY

1. The Book of Ruth, a well-known love story, is one of the greatest prosperity stories of all times.

2. This great story brings a message of hope to those people who have suffered sorrow, because it shows that there are always returning cycles when the good that seemed lost returns again in a new guise.

3. Ruth is placed in importance along with the millionaires of Genesis because she became the Bible's first millionairess through her own actions.

4. The story begins when Naomi and her husband left Bethlehem because of a famine there and went into the Land of Moab where hardships followed.

5. Her mistake was in leaving Bethlehem because it symbolizes a prosperous state of mind.

6. Naomi symbolizes every person who learns about the power of prosperous thinking, yet in times of distress, does not use it. She symbolizes those people, who in the face of lack, try to find an easy way out by going off to the Land of Moab.

7. Once you know how to use the power of thought constructively, no other method works for solving your problems. If you try to revert to former methods of rushing around, trying to make things right in outward ways, the situation only gets worse.

8. It never gets better until, like Naomi, you return to Bethlehem or begin to use the inner laws of prosperity again.

9. The word "Bethlehem" means "house of substance." You can return to the prosperous Bethlehem state of mind and reap its vast benefits by quietly inviting the powerful, loving substance of the universe into your life. Remarkable things happen when you practice doing this daily.

10. Ruth, symbolizing one who loves the inner world of mind and Spirit, accompanied Naomi to Bethlehem, where she became a gleaner in the fields of the rich Boaz. When she became willing to gather her good bit by bit, it multiplied.

11. Boaz, the Bethlehem millionaire, symbolizes prosperity at its best. He knew the prospering power of blessing people, places and things. He did it constantly.

12. After returning to the prosperous Bethlehem state of mind, Naomi did what we must all do next to demonstrate prosperity: She got specific by arranging a marriage between Ruth and Boaz, based on family ties. Her method worked. After prolonged poverty, she and Ruth became two of the richest and most beloved women in the city. Her sorrow had turned to joy. As you, too, use these methods you can demonstrate a Boaz in your life, or "prosperity at its best."

THE AUTHOR'S FINAL MESSAGE TO YOU

"You will enjoy the companion book to this one entitled
THE PROSPERITY SECRET OF THE AGES. That book
describes the over-all prosperity secrets found throughout
the book of Genesis, and it has inspired and prospered thousands.

"You will also enjoy other books in this continuing series
on THE MILLIONAIRES OF THE BIBLE, including
THE MILLIONAIRE MOSES, *His Prosperity Secrets For
You*, THE MILLIONAIRE JOSHUA, *His Prosperity
Secrets For You* and others to come."